SELVING

A RELATIONAL THEORY OF SELF ORGANIZATION

SELVING

A RELATIONAL THEORY OF SELF ORGANIZATION

Irene Fast

THE ANALYTIC PRESS

1998   Hillsdale, NJ   London

Published by The Analytic Press, Inc.
Editorial Offices: 101 West Street, Hillsdale, NJ 07642

Typeset by CompuDesign, Rego Park, NY

LIBRARY OF CONGRESS CATALOGING-IN-PUBLICATION DATA

Fast, Irene
  Selving : a relational theory of self organization / Irene Fast..
    p. cm
  Includes bibliographical references and index.
  ISBN 0-88163-206-6
  1. Psychoanalysis. 2. Self. 3. Freud, Sigmund,   1856-
1939.
I. Title.
BF175.D24   1998
155.2—dc21   97-51906
                                 CIP

Printed in the United States of America
10 9 8 7 6 5 4 3 2 1

ACKNOWLEDGMENTS

It is not possible, of course, to thank all the friends and colleagues who have contributed to working out the ideas in this book. I do want to mention by name, however, Jonathan Slavin, who has enthusiastically supported this work from its beginnings in event theory. It was Anne Thompson who suggested this specific project: a formulation of the dynamic self in event theory terms. I am enormously indebted to them and to Stephen Behnke, Philip Blumberg, Daniel Greenberg, and Brian Litzenberger, who have read and reread drafts of chapters, have offered suggestions, and have been steady sources of encouragement. From outside the psychoanalytic community, Ingrid Harms has been an invaluable source of support in her reading of chapter drafts for their accessibility to general readers and in enlarging my thinking with intriguing suggestions of linkages between the ideas presented here and those emerging from other arenas of thought. Finally, I want to thank my editor and publisher, Paul Stepansky, for his initial welcome of this project and his consistent availability for editorial review, useful suggestions, and necessary comfort.

CONTENTS

PREFACE

The notion of "I" permeates our daily lives. It speaks to our personally motivated ways of perceiving, thinking, feeling and acting: I see . . . I believe. . . . I remember . . . I think . . . I am going to. . . . . It is central, too, to psychoanalytic clinical work: therapeutic progress occurs as we integrate disavowed or ego alien experiences into our autobiographical selves. We make the difficult transitions from feeling a "wave" of anxiety, an inescapable "urge" to eat, or an overwhelming "need" to put ourselves in danger, to a sense of our feelings and thoughts and actions as our own.

Freud captured this contrast in his concepts of *das Ich* and *das Es*. In his clinically near formulations, both are organizations of personally motivated feelings, thoughts, and actions. *Ich* activities carry a conscious sense of I-ness; *Es* activities do not. Following the scientific *Zeitgeist* of his day, however, Freud structured his higher order theories in impersonal terms: *das Ich* and *das Es* became energy systems, no longer the personally motivated *Ich* and *Es* of his clinical observations. The notion of I-ness receded to the background.

In the influential formulations of ego psychology the dynamic "I" disappeared altogether. In that framework, our selves are not dynamic organizations The self is exclusively a self representation coordinate to object representations. Our ways of being tender toward a child, envying someone's abilities, and working to succeed in a career are not I-activities. They are fundamentally products of impersonal energic forces.

Curiously, object relations perspectives, aiming to take more fully into account people's relationships with one another, did not find a way to conceptualize our interactions as personal engagements. The basic building blocks of experience in major relational conceptions are self-other units of which the self and object aspects are representations. People's ways of relating, their ways of loving a friend, being afraid of an authority, or condemning a wrong-doer are not I-activities. The dynamic I-self does not easily find a place in these frameworks.

It seemed to me, increasingly, that we needed a new way of looking at the notion of a dynamic self. To be satisfactory, such a framework must be able to account for the observations Freud conceptualized as *das Ich* and *das Es.*. It must also be able to accommodate the rich bodies of observation that have emerged from ego psychology and object relations perspectives. It seemed to me, finally, that to whatever extent possible, it must also provide bridges to other domains of inquiry, both within psychology and outside it.

The notion of the "event," elaborated previously (Fast, 1985), seemed to offer possibilities for meeting these requirements. In that work, I proposed events as the basic units of experience and mental representation. Event schemes are patterned in personally motivated self–world engagements. They are dynamic schemes. They are related to self and object representations in definable ways. They develop through integration and differentiation. To examine the usefulness of this framework, my colleagues and I explored ways that thinking in event terms might illuminate aspects of primary narcissism and borderline disorders, primary and secondary process thought, boundary formation and loss, affect development and maturity in affective expression (Fitzpatrick, 1985; Thompson, 1985) of primitive thought forms (Erard, 1985), and omnipotence and primary creativity (Young and Fast, 1985).

It seemed that event schemes might also usefully be explored as the basic structures of our I-selves, as I-schemes. In their structure as schemes of personally motivated activity, they meet the defining criterion for being constituents of a dynamic self. Previous work had suggested that their structure could provide a useful way to reframe significant aspects of the primitive experience modes that classical theory attributes to the id or unconscious and to the transitions from id to ego. In their structure as interaction schemes and their development through integration and differentiation, they seemed also to provide possibilities for accommodating observations rooted in relational perspectives.

In this book I pursue that possibility. It is an attempt to show how the structure of I-schemes and their development might accommodate clinical observations and conceptions made within traditional and relational perspectives in psychoanalysis. I begin with the basic psychoanalytic assumption that all psychologically relevant experience is personally motivated and is, therefore, self experience. A *sense* of I-ness, however, accompanies our activities (perceiving, thinking, feeling, acting) only to the extent that our I-schemes are integrated and differentiated. To that extent, too, our activities have the characteristics attributed to the ego in classical theory and to whole self, whole object relations in relational perspectives. To the extent that I-schemes are not integrated, activities carry little sense of I-ness and are characterized by id phenomena and by part-self, part-object relationships. I refer to all self activities, with or without a *sense* of I-ness, as "selving," to emphasize their active, dynamic character.

I illustrate ways in which this conception of our I-selves might be relevant to psychoanalytic thought, in the context, both of well-known clinical observations and related, clinically near conceptions, and of current clinical and theoretical controversies. Among the former are suggestions for ways we might usefully rethink our notions about the persistence of early ways of selving in later life: introjective–projective activities in development and adult defensive activity; the patterning of "as-if" phenomena and screen identities; characteristics of reality testing; the establishment of our inner worlds of intrapsychic

activity and their loss in patterns of "acting out"; and the structure of transference–countertransference relationships and their
resolution.

Significant current debates are being stimulated especially by
the growing ascendancy of relational perspectives in this country. The idea of our dynamic selves as constellations of interactive I-schemes suggests ways we might think about the place of
body-based experience in a relational model; intrapsychic organizations that are also relational; the coexistence of individuality
and relationship in interactions; primitive and sophisticated
structures of intersubjectivity; the places of repression and dissociation in a relational conception; and the coexistence of
coherence and multiplicity in our self structures.

In the course of this work it was borne in on me, increasingly,
that the notion of I-schemes, schemes of selving, as the basic
structures of our dynamic selves is congruent with developing
directions of inquiry both within psychoanalysis and outside it.
Within clinical psychoanalysis, it is in tune with the large body
of Loewald's (1980) conceptions from within classical drive theory; with Kernberg's (1966) attempts at a framework that
accommodates both drive and relational perspectives; with
Schafer's (1976) action language; and with Ogden's (1986) conceptions rooted in the Kleinian tradition. Its major base outside
psychoanalytic psychology is Piaget's (Flavell, 1963) conception
of action schemes and their development by integration and differentiation. It is in tune with current findings in infancy research
and, specifically, with Stern's (1985) GERs as basic units of self
structure, and with the interaction structures that Beebe and her
colleagues (1997) propose to account for early infant–mother
interactions. More generally, it is in accord with trends that seem
increasingly to move away from the Cartesian objectivist tradition, toward one that conceives of our minds as organizations of
subjective, personally motivated interaction structures, such as
the Internal Working Models that Fonagy and his colleagues
(1993) explore; the schemes Nelson (1986) proposes, from the
standpoint of developmental psychology, to account for the

ways children represent their activities mentally; the metaphoric projections Lakoff and Johnson (1980), from their bases in linguistics and philosophy, respectively, propose as central to mental activity; and the structures of Dasein explored in work rooted in Heidegger's philosophy (Dreyfus, 1991).

The form of this work is schematic. I have wanted to present a few central ideas as clearly as possible and to illuminate some of their implications by placing them in a variety of contexts. The major theoretical perspectives are those of classical and object relations theories. For strategic purposes I highlight facets of the I-self conception quite starkly against fundamental aspects of these approaches, with the hope that the gain in clarity can make up for the loss of richness that would accompany more nuanced discussion. I have chosen, too, to speak to a wide variety of psychoanalytic issues in only enough detail to suggest directions for further exploration, rather than more intensively addressing major bodies of thought (e.g., gender organization, structure of primitive part-self, part-object structures to id phenomena, and implications of the I-self conception for psychoanalytic technique). It seems to me that such issues require their own separate, more intensive exploration. Aspects of selving are illustrated with a wide variety of clinical examples, but I also use a few of them repeatedly, in context after context, as nuclear examples that might help the reader draw together diverse aspects of the I-self notion. Empirical data from various domains are adduced where they might contribute to the clarification of one or another idea.

Psychoanalytic psychology and, especially, relational perspectives within it are currently bursting with vitality. In this exciting time, we can expect that a variety of theories and part-theories will be proposed to address questions about how we might imagine our dynamic selves. The I-self framework is intended as one of these. If we are fortunate, we will, over time, forge a broadly acceptable consensus about our dynamic selves, perhaps one that hearkens back to, though it will surely also differ from, Freud's seminal conception of our *Ich*.

SELVING

A RELATIONAL THEORY OF SELF ORGANIZATION

1 TOWARD THE NOTION OF A DYNAMIC I-SELF

In 1892, William James proposed a way of understanding the self that powerfully shaped self exploration in the succeeding 100 years. He suggested that we think of the self as composed of two major aspects, the self as me and the self as I.

The me-self, or self as object, refers to our self representations. One's me-self might include a current sense of oneself as parent or psychologist, one's remembered self as a seventh-grader, half-hidden notions of oneself as doomed to loneliness or as somehow incomplete, idealized images of oneself as totally good, a fantasied self as tennis star, or dream images of self as circus clown or white-coated scientist. The me-self is the self observed in self observation.

The I-self is the self as subject. It is the observer in self observation. The I-self is dynamic. It includes our ways of perceiving, thinking, feeling, remembering, imagining, acting. It is the self aspect of "I think . . . ," "I am going to . . . ," "I feel like . . . ," "I remember . . ."

The idea that the self has these two aspects remains fundamental to academic and psychoanalytic psychologies alike.
Already in 1892 James found the I-self much more difficult to
identify and describe than the me-self. It is a difficulty still unresolved in academic psychology and is one we are only begining
to address in psychoanalytic psychology.

Hartmann: Only Self Representations Are Self

In psychoanalytic psychology, the notion of the self as representational has dominated our conceptions. Hartmann (1950) set
the stage for its centrality in the distinction he made between
self and ego. Freud had used the term *Ich* (self) to refer to both,
but, beginning in the 1930s, in the context of the new ego psychology, confusions of self and ego posed constant problems of
clarity of thought in clinical work and theory development. A
focus on the ego as one part of the id-ego-superego systems
could not accommodate the notion of the ego as the self, with its
implication of individuals in interaction with their human and
nonhuman worlds. Conversely, the ego as the self could not be
squeezed into the confines of the ego identified as one of the three
dynamic systems of the structural model.

Hartmann proposed a widely valued solution to this problem.
He suggested that ego and self be seen as terms relevant to different domains of discourse: the ego was to be viewed as a structure
of impersonal dynamic functions coordinate to the id and the
superego of Freud's structural model; self was to be construed as
a self representation coordinate to object representations.

Hartmann's conception of the ego cleared away confusions
about the meanings of that term and set the stage for his and his
colleagues' prodigious work in the development of ego psychology. The implications of his conception for the study of self were
also momentous. In its immediate effect, his notion of the self as

a self representation helped to organize and clarify a wide range of clinical observations, particularly as psychoanalytic clinicians and theory makers interested themselves more and more in object relations. Among those who expressed their gratitude to Hartmann for this useful distinction in encouraging exploration of self representations were such major figures as Jacobson (1964), Sandler and Rosenblatt (1961), Kernberg (1966), Modell (1968), and Schafer (1976).

In investigations that followed, self and object representations tended to be conceived as initially fused or merged with one another and as gradually achieving independence. Primitive self and object representations observed clinically began to be seen as part-selves and part-objects, which, for various reasons, were not integrated into a whole self and whole objects. The projection and introjection of self and object representations observed in the pathologies of adulthood were traced to normal alternations of introjection and projection in the childhood development of self and object representations. Developmental progressions were traced from introjects to identifications and the gradual establishment of capabilities for self observation.

In this conception, the dynamic processes of the id-ego-superego systems affect self representations in the same way that they influence object representations, distorting them in various ways, interfering with the development from part-selves to a whole self, or resulting in the persistence of primitive introjective and projective processes and the incomplete differentiation of self and object.

But what of the self as subject, the I-self? In psychoanalytic psychology, the cognitive, conative, and affective processes that James ascribed to the I-self constitute the dynamic aspects of the mind. They are the processes Freud included in his model of the id, ego, and superego. Can we agree with James's view of these dynamic processes as self activities? Hartmann et al. (1947) argued strongly that we cannot. In their view, the dynamic aspects of the mind must not be seen as self aspects. They are *impersonal* functions. In our theoretical thinking, we must *not* speak of our id passions, our ego activities, our ways of approving of or criticizing ourselves as personal actions rather than as impersonal functions. If we do so, we introduce an unacceptable anthropomorphism into the theory. We apply personal motivations to what are, in fact, functions subject to impersonal laws.[1]

Here the conception of Hartmann and his colleagues has influenced psychoanalytic explorations of self in two ways that have proven less useful. First, his conception of the self as nondynamic, as restricted to self representations, flies in the face of experience and of Freud's own use of the term *Ich* ('I'). In our personal and clinical experience, our selves are manifestly involved in dynamic functions. They are central to our loving someone, taking pride in an achievement, envying a rival, criticizing ourselves, imagining a desired future, remembering a childhood pleasure, or working toward a goal. For Hartmann and his colleagues, these are not self activities—they are expressions of impersonal forces. self aspects are no more than representations. A representation does not love, take pride, envy, admire, imagine, or remember.

Hartmann and colleagues' conception of self as only a representation is also incompatible with Freud's *Ich* as self. Freud's *Ich* is dynamic. It comprises our ways of seeking compromises between id and superego, actualizing our goals in the external world, defending ourselves against anxieties, and finding ways to satisfy our wishes in acceptable ways. The dynamic superego, too, is a self function (*das Überich*), in which one self aspect criticizes or praises another. The place of the self in id processes is less clear. Freud seems at some times to describe them as physiological forces without self content, but, at others, he appears to identify them as physiologically based impulses expressed psychologically as disavowed wishes with that term's implication of personal motivation rather than impersonal causation.

---

[1] Schafer's (1976) "action language" for psychoanalysis can be seen to be in vigorous opposition to Hartmann's widely held position. In Schafer's view, all mental events, all subjective activities, are personal and agentic. They are constructions of human agency rather than impersonal happenings.

To Freud's thinking, moreover, the idea that *all* psychological processes are personally motivated is fundamental. Our ways of loving, taking pride, envying, and imagining are all personally motivated. Every impulse, wish, symptom fragment, masturbatory ritual, dream, or action is an expression of personal wishes, aims, fears, avoidances, or self criticisms. All psychological development and clinical change reflects individuals' personal resolutions of conflicting wishes and aims, with their associated thoughts, feelings and actions. In Freud's conceptions close to his clinical base, and in our common experience but not in Hartmann's framework, James's dynamic I-self could find a ready place.

In a second, somewhat less obvious way, Hartmann's restriction of self to mean self representation has proven a significant obstacle to clinical understanding and theory development. The idea of self strongly invites a relational conception in which self and other are coordinate to one another. It invites notions that when we try to accomplish something we are interacting with our worlds, that our feelings of tenderness occur in relationships, that our self criticisms are interactions between two aspects of self. It is an idea that occurs in Freud's work (e.g., 1914, 1921), but not one he elaborated extensively. Hartmann's emphasis on the dynamic aspects of our minds as impersonal forces cannot easily accommodate an interactional perspective. In his view, striving to accomplish, feeling tenderly, or criticizing ourselves are not fundamentally activities of our selves in relation to our worlds. They are, at root, expressions of the impersonal forces within people that constitute the id, ego, and superego.

Hartmann's idea of self representations as coordinate to object representations might suggest a relational approach. And, indeed, the major developments emerging from his distinction of self and ego have a strong object relational flavor. In Hartmann's own conception, however, self and object representations are not structured in ways that entail, or easily accommodate, relationships. A self representation, in his view, is structured in the same way as an object representation. Both begin as mental registrations of sensory impressions. Once registered in the mind, they may be in various ways modified by the drives. Self and object representations defined as perceptual registrations modified by impersonal functions do not easily accommodate notions of self–other relationships.

Toward Conceptions of a Dynamic Self

Currently a growing thrust of clinical and theoretical thinking in psychoanalytic psychology is directed toward ideas in tune with James's notion of the dynamic I-self. Moreover, in psychoanalytic perspectives, though not explicitly in James's work, this I-self is consistently seen in relational terms.

The very notion of a dynamic self is at odds with our usual ways of thinking. We ordinarily speak of having a self that acts in various ways, perceiving, thinking, feeling, or observing itself. But if we think of id, ego, and superego processes as self functions, we must consider another possibility. Our thinking, feeling, and acting are not what our self *does*; they are what our self *is*. It is not that our self loves, takes pride, envies, imagines, and remembers: our loving, taking pride, envying, imagining, and remembering *are* self.

James (1892) faces this issue head-on. The notion of an I-self invites the idea of an entity that acts in certain ways. But that is not James's intent. He asks whether, in thinking about the I-self, we must think of a substantial self that thinks and feels and wills, or whether the thinking and the feelings are themselves self. He opts for the latter. Philosophers, James observes, often postulate a Thinker or Agent that does the thinking or perceiving or feeling. It seems to them that the multitudinous and transient impulses that characterize our experience cannot account for our feelings of identity at a particular moment and over time. But, James argues, the notion of a Thinker or Agent only pushes the problem of identity back a step. We are now faced with the problem of how this entity might provide the continuity and identity that we experience in the I-self. Better, he suggests, that we find the identity of the I-self in the processes themselves, the ways they are integrated into the unified experience of a present moment, and the ways the remembered past provides a sense of identity over time.

We do not need to postulate an I-self who thinks and feels and knows. It is the thinking itself, the feeling, and the willing that *are* the I-self.

Kegan (1982) also elaborates this attractive but difficult idea. He suggests that we are tempted by our language to experience our selves, as we do the rest of the world, as things that act: we each have a self that does various things. He argues that we must resist that temptation. We must think of self as an activity rather than as a thing. We tend to think of ourselves as human beings, he writes, but we might better think of our selves as our ways of being human. His aim is to explore the evolving self, not as the doing that a self *does*, but the doing that a self *is*.

Put another way, if we are to think of the dynamic aspects of the mind as self, we must find ways to think of self, not in terms of nouns and adjectives, but in terms of verbs and adverbs. We must learn to think of ourselves not as having a self, but of doing self things or, for lack of a more suitable word, perhaps of "selving."

This perspective is not altogether unfamiliar to psychoanalytic psychology. Freud did not propose a self that does things. Freud's *Ich* is itself dynamic. It comprises our ways of thinking, defending ourselves against anxiety, working toward accomplishments, and so forth. It is not an *Ich* that *does* these things— these doings *are Ich*; they *are* our selves.[2]

---

[2] Jacobson (1997) makes a similar point in his illuminating discussion of Christopher Bollas's work. He questions the need for postulating an endogenous "true self" or "idiom core" that we strive to realize in our interactions with our worlds, rather than finding our personal idioms in the patternings of our self–world interactions themselves.

Can we argue that we are "selving" when we are loving someone, watching the rain, or remembering an ancient shame? Can we find ways to conceive these processes and all the others we familiarly consider aspects of id, ego, and superego as self activities? Can we do so, keeping in mind that we must also account for self representations (the me-self) in relation to the dynamic I-self, and that in psychoanalytic frameworks the notion of self tends to occur in the context of self–other relationships? This is the case that must be made, I believe, if we are to think of the dynamic processes of the mind as the I-self.

It will not be easy. Our language and thought forms so dominate our usage that we are virtually compelled to notions of the self as a subject that does various things. Already in the foregoing, "the self" has been referrred to more than once. And in the rest of this book, that will happen often. It may be that we will have to satisfy ourselves with an uneasy truce in which, on one hand, we accept that speaking of "the self" is perhaps inevitable; but, on the other, we remain alert to remember that we are speaking of a constellation of activities.

Attempts to Formulate Id and Ego Activities as Self

In psychoanalytic psychology we are in the early stages of our attempts to find ways to account for the I-self and its relationships in terms of the "doings" that Freud framed in his structural model, particularly of the id and ego. Nevertheless, these ideas are taking interesting directions.

Kernberg (1966) approaches the problem in the context of his clinical observations of borderline character organization. He observed that his patients seemed to split their experience into disparate states, altogether irreconcilable with one another. At one moment, for example, a patient might experience himself with Kernberg as a rejected, depreciated little boy in relation to a harsh and haughty adult; at another, as a longing, guilt-ridden child with an all-forgiving, all-loving grown-up. The two states seemed altogether distinct. The patient could hardly remember his positive views of Kernberg when feeling negatively toward him, and when he idealized Kernberg he could hardly recall his earlier negative views.

Each of these discrete states seemed to Kernberg to represent a complete transference paradigm in which a specific object relationship was activated. It was as if they were discrete ego states, almost like two selves completely separated in their emotions. It was Kernberg's sense that these relationship units were pathologically fixed remnants of the normal processes of early development. These observations led him to a novel conception. The basic organizations that structure our minds, he proposes, are dynamic interaction units composed of a self aspect and an object aspect linked by an affect. From such relationship units the id, ego, and superego processes as well as object relationships develop.

Could these basic structures of the mind, these ways of interacting with the world be units of self structure? When the patient feels like a rejected little boy before a haughty adult or longs for the all-forgiving Kernberg, is this an I-self activity? Kernberg suggests that possibility in his clinical discussion: the patient's nonmetabolized ego states seemed to him like two selves separated from one another. If these dyadic units could be construed as selves (part-selves), or I-self units, we might have a base for constructing a model for a dynamic I-self that accommodates both the phenomena included in the structural model and those of object relations perspectives.

In his theoretical discussion, however, Kernberg leaves this clinically based idea behind. Instead, he fully accepts Hartmann's theoretical strictures: when the patient yearns for Kernberg's love or feels guilty he is not selving. The affects (of yearning or guilt) that link self and object representations are fundamentally impersonal drive structures.

Given his commitment to Hartmann's views, Kernberg cannot follow his clinical intuition that his patient's disparate ways of interacting with him are expressions of his I-self. He cannot pursue the possibility that the I-self occurs initially in interaction units, the infant's ways of engaging its world. He is prevented from considering the possibility that it is from such dynamic units of I-self experience that object relations and id, ego, and superego functions develop.

Meissner (1986) approaches the question of the I-self directly. He argues that it is a significant lack in psychoanalytic theory not to have a clear way of accounting for people's feelings of agency and their sense of "I." The notion of the self as exclusively a self representation is unsatisfactory. We need a concept of self that includes both the self as a representation and the dynamic self as subject. Meissner's goal is to conceptualize the dynamic self in a way that accommodates the id, ego, and superego functions of the structural theory

Like Kernberg, however, Meissner remains altogether committed to Hartmann's views. He argues, following Hartmann, that we cannot simply equate the dynamic self with the id, ego, and superego of the structural theory. Strictly speaking, he writes, the "structural entities (the id, ego, and superego) do not imply any specific personal reference. They are organizations of impersonal functions" (p. 389). He proposes a superordinate self that "embraces and includes the contributions of the id, ego, and superego" (p. 380) and also provides a base for object relations perspectives. It is this superordinate self that organizes the impersonal functions of the id, ego, and superego into such complex experiences as a patient's sense of guilt, yearning for love, or feelings of rejection and depreciation and endows them with feelings of personal agency and I-ness.

The notion of a superordinate self, however, faces all the problems that James found in the notion of Thinkers and Agents that philosophers posit to account for the sense of identity they cannot find in the dynamic processes of the mind themselves. It only pushes the problem back a step. Now we must account for our sense of personal agency and I-ness in our activities by way of this new superordinate self. It is a problem that, thus far, has not been solved.

In disagreement with Hartmann, Eagle (1984a) commits himself firmly to the idea that all the dynamic functions of the mind are self functions. All perceptions, thoughts, feelings, and actions are personally motivated. The dynamic functions Freud included in his conceptions of id, ego, and superego are, in this view, those James included in the I-self.

This commitment leads Eagle directly to a question that James did not consider but that is central to psychoanalytic psychology. If we are to consider all dynamic aspects of our minds as personally motivated, how shall we distinguish those thoughts, perceptions, feelings, and actions that people feel as their own (Freud's *das Ich* or ego) from those they experience as ego alien (*das Es*, the id)

Eagle suggests that in considering that issue we commonly conflate two theoretical positions. The first is Hartmann's ego-psychological view. From that perspective, both ego and id are seen as structures of impersonal functions. The id is a reservoir of biologically based instinctual forces unrelated to reality that threaten us with the feeling that we might be overwhelmed by powers that we cannot identify and understand. The ego, powered by the same impersonal, biologically based energies, controls these chaotic forces and channels them toward orderly and adaptive ends.

In the second view, both id and ego are self aspects. The ego, *das Ich*, refers to those of our thoughts, feelings, and actions that we experience as parts of ourselves. The id, *das Es*, refers to personally motivated thoughts, feelings, and actions that we disown as not-self.

In a common conflation of these two views, Eagle suggests, the ego is identified with personal wishes, urges, plans, and so forth that individuals accept as their own. Only the id is seen as a reservoir of biologically based impersonal experience.

Eagle urges that we think entirely in terms of the second of the two formulations. Both ego and id are, in a basic sense,

grounded in biological processes. Both, as they occur psychologically, refer to personal motivations, cognitions, and perceptions. The distinction between id and ego is not between self
and not-self—all motivations are self. Ego and id are distinguished by people's acceptance of their activities as their own
and their experience of them as ego alien, respectively.

This view, Eagle suggests, gives rise to a conception of persons as attempting to carry out a variety of aims, some in conflict with each other and others in harmony, some infantile and
others more mature, and all with varying degrees of personal
acknowledgment and conscious awareness. In such a view, he
argues, Freud's dictum "where id was, there shall ego be" does
not refer to people's increased control over their infantile
instinctual impulses, but to their increased ownership and avowal
of disclaimed wishes and aims. What was disowned and experienced as impersonal comes to be owned and experienced as
part of oneself.

Loewald (1980) elaborates similar views in an explicitly
interactional perspective. Like Eagle, he fully rejects Hartmann's
argument that the dynamic functions of the mind must be seen
to be impersonal forces. In his view, on the contrary, it is a fundamental tenet of psychoanalysis that all that transpires psychically is personally motivated. He emphasizes, more strongly
than Eagle does, that these personal motivations are rooted in
instincts that are themselves structured interpersonally: "Instincts,
understood as psychic, motivational forces, become organized
as such through interactions within a psychic field consisting
originally of the mother–child psychic unit" (pp. 127–128).

Like Eagle, Loewald differentiates the id and ego in terms of
those processes people experience as automatic or intrusions
from outside, on one hand, and actions they experience as personal, on the other. In his view, motivation becomes increasingly personalized as people make progress in development or
clinical work. In analysis, for example, a woman plagued by a
compulsion to murder her child might begin to understand that
the feelings of hate she harbors toward the child are connected

to a disturbed relationship with her husband and, in turn, to feelings toward her father (Loewald, 1980). That is, what she experienced as an impersonal, compelling force becomes part of the network of the interpersonally structured motivations that constitute her self.

Although Loewald emphasizes throughout that all psychic processes are personally motivated, he prefers to reserve the term self for those which individuals themselves experience as I-activities. He refers to unconscious processes as "potentially personal." A person becomes more fully a self when he or she begins to repeat with awareness ways of doing things that have previously been repeated automatically. The life of the individual, he suggests, "has the potential of being conducted by the person himself, . . . the course and conduct of one's life, within certain limits, can be, or can be helped to be in one's own hands" (p. 105).

Ogden (1986) begins outside the orbit of Hartmann's conceptions, within those of Melanie Klein. He proposes, with Kernberg, that the basic structures of our minds are dynamic self–other units. Ogden, however, identifies these units with the self quite differently than Kernberg does in his formal, Hartmann-influenced theory. He does not suggest that the self aspect of an interaction unit is only a nondynamic self representation. Rather, if I read Ogden correctly, he suggests, in ways that resonate with Loewald's conceptions, that self–other units themselves—our ways of going at things—constitute our I-selves. Ogden describes them as codes or templates[3] by which we understand our experience and act in our worlds, whether lovingly, suspiciously, trustingly, or enviously. All these interpersonally patterned activities are I-activities.

In Ogden's view, to use Kernberg's clinical example, the patient's self is not limited to his self representation as a

---

[3] The terms code and template illuminate the ways these self–other units pattern our thinking, feeling, and acting. Readers must be careful to avoid the erroneous implication that, in Ogden's view, they are static structures, as templates or codes typically are, rather than dynamic ones.

rejected, depreciated little boy. The patient's entire way of interacting with Kernberg as a rejected little boy in relation to a harsh
and haughty adult is a self activity. It is the expression of a long-
established interaction template that he now actualizes in the
transference.

Like Eagle and Loewald, Ogden is centrally interested in differentiating events in which people have an experience of I-ness
and agency and those in which they do not. He follows Klein in
ascribing the first to the depressive mode, the second to the
paranoid-schizoid one. In experience typical of the depressive
period, the sense of I-ness is central. People have a sense of personal aliveness in their ways of going at things. They feel themselves to be the interpreters of their perceptions. Events do not
just happen: they are what one makes of them.

In the paranoid-schizoid mode, as in the depressive one, people understand and act in their worlds in terms of the codes or
templates that pattern their ways of going at things. They do so,
however, without a sense of either self or agency. As Ogden
writes about infant experience, "From an outsider's point of
view, the infant interprets perceptions in, for example, a para-
noid or loving way. The infant, however, has no awareness of
himself as interpreter of experience" (p. 27). In the paranoid-
schizoid experience of adulthood, events are not what one
makes of them but, rather, are things that happen to one: an anxiety "attack," a "wave" of depression, or an irresistible "need" to
binge, to take drugs, or to put oneself in physical danger.

The sense of I-ness in one's experience is a developmental or
clinical accomplishment. In a patient's transition from the paranoid-schizoid to the depressive mode, for example, "What had
been something happening to the patient (a need to binge)
became her wish (to eat in a particular way)" (p. 118).

These conceptions are central to Ogden's sensitively detailed
elaborations of people's functioning. At times, however, he
appears to take a different view, one in which, like that of the
philosophers in James's account, the self is an entity separate
from its actions. In one place, for example, he locates I-ness in

"the psychological space in which one thinks one's thoughts, lives in one's body, dreams one's dreams . . ." (p. 42n). In another he suggests that "I" is "the interpreter of one's symbols, the mediator between one's thoughts and that which one is thinking about, the intermediary between the self and one's lived sensory experience" (p. 72).

In such views, the I-self does not exist in the activities of thinking, dreaming, or immersing oneself in sensory experience; it is a separate self that does these things. In Kegan's (1982) terms, these are the doings that the self *does*, not the doings that the self *is*. As in the case of Meissner's (1986) superordinate self, such ideas pose the unresolved problem of delineating a self separate from its activities. They are sufficiently present in Ogden's work to require noting, but they figure little in the complexities of his discussions. Those identify self with the interactional units that are the patterns by which we think and feel and act in our worlds.

In these attempts to formulate a psychoanalytic conception of the I-self that accommodates the processes Freud included in his structural model of the mind, we can see a gradual move away from Hartmann's requirements that self be seen only as a representation and that the dynamic aspects of our minds be understood to be impersonal forces. Increasingly, in tune with James and Kegan, we seem to be moving from a notion of a self that does various things toward a view that the dynamic processes themselves are I-activities. The I-self is coming to be understood, not as one aspect of an interaction, but as the interaction mode itself, one's ways of going at things, the codes or templates by which one understands and interacts with one's world. In that context, growing attention is being paid to problems of differentiating those self activities that people accept as their own and those they find ego alien.

As we move toward a satisfactory framework for understanding the dynamic aspects of the mind as self aspects, we invite a host of challenging questions. How might we most usefully formulate the interaction units that constitute the I-self? Shall we include all interaction units in the I-self, or shall we, like Loewald (1980), reserve the term self for those activities that individuals themselves experience as I-activities? In what ways are self representations (the me-self), easily forgotten in our new concentration on the I-self, related to the dynamic I-self? Can we define id, ego, and superego functions as self activities without the anthropomorphism that Hartmann thought must accompany any attempt to view those functions as personal actions? Can we show how significant aspects of human functioning understood in id and ego terms find a place in notions that interaction units defined as I-activities are the basic units of the mind? Can we delineate these interaction units in such a way that they also accommodate object relational notions of part-selves and part-objects, the differentiation and integration of self and other, processes of introjection and projection, and so forth?

We can expect that, as we continue to deal with these problems and others, an increasing array of theories and part theories will be proposed to accommodate more and more fully our clinical observations and theoretical commitments. The aim of this book is to provide one such framework.

A Preview

I propose two criteria for identifying activities (perceiving, thinking, feeling, and acting) as self activities: the presence of personal agency and the individual's own sense of "I." Of the two, personal agency is primary.

Thus, for example, peristaltic activity, the widening of the pupil in response to light, and the bowel movements of early infancy are not self. Perhaps for most people peristaltic activity never becomes a self aspect. The widening of the pupil can, however, be brought under one's own control, and most people learn to regulate the place and time of their bowel evacuations in early childhood. These, then, become self activities.

Agentic activity may or may not be accompanied by a subjective sense of self. As clinicians have long believed and formal
research is increasingly demonstrating (Demos, 1992), children's activities are agentic (purposive) from the beginning of
life. From the time of birth, therefore, people are engaged in self
activity. Only in the course of development, however, do people become self aware. Use of the personal pronoun "I" at
about age two signals major achievements in that process. In
adulthood, people's ways of excluding agentic activities from
their I-experience, and the complexities of the clinical processes
by which they come to include them as self activities, are central to clinical psychoanalysis. They are fundamental to discussions of id and ego, processes of defense, and the nature of
therapeutic action.

In succeeding chapters I pursue the idea that all the dynamic
aspects of our minds are agentic. They are personal motivations
rather than impersonal functions; they constitute James's (1982)
I-self of thinking, feelings and willing. In Kegan's (1982) terms,
these activities are not the doings that the self *does*, but the
doings that the self *is*. It is a conception that remains true to
Freud's conviction that *all* psychological processes are personally motivated: every perception, memory, wish, symptom fragment, and dream.

I suggest, with Loewald (1980) and Ogden (1986), that we
think of these I-self activities as our ways of interacting with our
worlds, whether in confident expectation of success, in suspi-
cious anticipation of rejection, or in easy assurance that our
affection will be reciprocated. With Ogden, I suggest that these
activities take the form of interaction schemes, and these interaction schemes, in turn, become the patterns (in Ogden's terms,
the templates or codes) by which we understand and act in our
worlds. I refer to them as I-schemes to maximize our sense of
them as dynamic.

I define these I-schemes as units of personally motivated
interaction between self and nonself. The dynamic phenomena
Freud included in his structural theory as well as those central

to object relations perspectives develop from these I-schemes. Their early structure as undifferentiated and unintegrated units without separation of thought and action gives rise to the phenomena that Freud ascribed to the id; here, however, they are identified as aspects of self structure and development. I-scheme development, by processes of integration and differentiation, leads, by about 18 to 24 months, to the phenomena Freud attributed to the child's turn to reality: the recognition of an external world independent of self and the ability to act in one's mind without accompanying bodily action. Here, too, the conception of the relevant processes as I-activities rather than impersonal drive functions provides altered perspectives on familiar conceptions.

The coordinate development of object relations is also rooted in the dynamic I-schemes. Initially, individual I-schemes reflect the interaction process itself, nursing, for example, without separate identification of the infant and the mother in the nursing interaction. In coordinate integration and differentiation processes, infants gradually distinguish the aspects of an interaction that belong to the mother from those of the self.

In those same processes, representations of self and other (e.g., of one's infant self and the mother) are gradually being distinguished from the activity itself. James's me-self is being established, and, coordinate to it, representations of others and of the nonhuman world. Throughout life, in this model, self and object representations and dynamic self schemes are intimately related: self and object representations at any given moment reflect precisely the dynamic schemes then in play.

This, in broad outline, is the program for this book.[4] Now,

---

[4] Daniel Greenberg (personal communication) has suggested that in significant ways the I-self conception is congruent with Heidegger's philosophy. My own reading of Heidegger, at second hand (Dreyfus, 1991), suggests that Greenberg may be right.

Heidegger was reacting strenuously against the Cartesian tradition in philosophy. In contrast to the notion of a relation between a self sufficient mind and an independent world (self and other), he proposed *Dasein*, our involved first, we turn to an articulation of the basic I-self structures from which all further development must proceed.

---

and active being-in-the-world. In his view, we are not essentially individual, autonomous, rational subjects; we are embodied, meaning-giving, doing subjects; we (our I-selves?) are our ways of *Daseining*. It is in *Daseining* (selving?) that we learn about our selves and our worlds. It is possible for us to learn as reflective, detached observers in scientific or other intellectual work, but that form of learning is derivative of the primary form that occurs in our active, embodied being-in-the-world.

The idea that a major direction of philosophical thought is significantly congruent with notions of the dynamic I-self explored in the more limited psychoanalytic arena is exciting. It suggests possibilities for wide-ranging expansions of the ideas presented here, in the light of Heidegger's own elaboration of this idea and that of others in his field, though their exploration may require philosophical sensibilities well beyond my own capacities.

2 BASIC STRUCTURES

In chapter 1 we saw a beginning convergence of ways in which we might usefully formulate units of I-self structure to accommodate the complex processes we typically include among the dynamic functions of the mind. In the clinical intuition that drove Kernberg's (1966) formulation, and more explicitly in the work of Loewald (1980) and Ogden (1986), we saw proposals for formulating the basic units of our dynamic selves as personally directed interactions between self and nonself that govern our ways of going about things in our worlds. This chapter delineates as fully as is currently possible one way of construing these basic self structures.[1]

---

[1] This conception of a dynamic self has origins in both psychoanalytic and Piagetian perspectives, and in an earlier attempt (Fast, 1985) to suggest one way to integrate them in a manner that accommodates both classical and relational perspectives in psychoanalysis. Russell's (1996) work provides an

I-Self Structures: Dynamic Schemes of Interaction

Any one of a number of infant activities could serve as an introductory example of I-self units: the infant's exchange of mutual gaze with the caregiver, watching a mobile above the crib, grasping its father's finger. The child nursing, an activity with many associations for psychoanalytically oriented readers, seems particularly useful.

In nursing, as in every other activity, this model proposes, the infant is actively engaged in an affective-cognitive-motoric interaction with its world. In the sense used here, it is selving, although with no implication that the infant has a *sense* of self. The nursing event is registered mentally as a nursing scheme. It is an I-scheme, a dynamic scheme of interaction. It is a scheme representing the infant's own way of going about its nursing activity in its world. It includes all the perceptive, cognitive, emotional and physical aspects of this personally motivated activity. Schemes such as this one, modified in the course of time, are basic to our ways of engaging our worlds: our ways of dealing with money, of understanding our colleagues, of enjoying a book. They lie at the root of the transference patterns we observe clinically. In Kegan's (1982) terms, they are what the self is, not what the self does.[2]

---

excellent exploration of Piagetian frameworks that, in its emphasis on the centrality of agency, the relationship of agency to a sense of one's identity, the origins of agency and identity in undifferentiated interaction schemes and their development by integration and differentiation, is in significant ways congruent with the one developed here.

[2] This view differs from the notion that we are object seeking. That term seems to have had its origins in Fairbairn's (1952) emphasis that relationships, rather than drive satisfaction, are central to people's lives. Hence, people are object seeking rather than pleasure seeking. To say that our selves are constituted by interaction schemes seems to serve Fairbairn's intent without the unwanted implication that we are solitary beings except as we seek and find relationships.

This concept of I-schemes is congruent in major ways with Stern's (1994) conception of a protonarrative envelope as the form in which lived experience is represented mentally. Moreover, Stern valuably emphasizes that every scheme is also a *temporal* unit. In a single episode of nursing, for example, we might see shifts in the strength of the activated motivation, in the quality of affect, in affect intensity, in hedonic tone. Stern refers to this as the temporal contour of feeling that unfolds while the motive is in play. In his view, this temporal feeling shape is the structural backbone of the lived moment, to which I refer as the event.

I-schemes are not constellations of mental representations. A nursing event might include the infant's active sucking, the smells of milk and mother, the mother's holding arm, the creak and movement of the rocker. It is registered mentally, however, as a scheme of action (a nursing scheme). The persons and objects of the event (the infant self, the mother, the rocker) are inchoate in the dynamic scheme. They contribute to the scheme's pattern, but they are not, at first, separately represented in the mind.[3]

The infant does not initially differentiate the self and not-self aspects of I-schemes. It does not distinguish its own contributions to the nursing episode from those of the mother: its own vigorous sucking, its gazing, or its postural adjustments from the part played by the mother's reciprocal gaze, her adjustments of breast or bottle, her holding activities, or her rocking. In later forms of this nondifferentiation, perhaps, a young mother feeds her baby when, in fact, it is she who is hungry; a greedy entre-

---

[3] Beebe, Lachmann, and Jaffe (1997), in the context of their studies of early infant–mother interactions, appear to be positing a similar mental structure. They suggest that presymbolic experience is represented mentally as the "dynamic interactive process itself" (p. 135), with no representation of self or other. In his discussion of their paper, Kulka (1997) vigorously endorses the idea that in early development an interaction is registered mentally "as an entity defined *not* by its components—the self and the other—but by the process of its own interactiveness" (p. 183).

preneur fears always that he is being robbed; an angry patient
feels that a threatening mood permeates the room.

Schemes are initially discrete. The still inchoate persons and
objects involved in them are defined in terms of the scheme in
which they occur. The nursing scheme has as its participants the
self-of-nursing, the rocker-of-nursing, the mother-of-nursing. In
other schemes, self and nonself are defined differently: the
mother-of-bye-bye; the self-of-cuddling-with-daddy. For the
infant, the mother-of-nursing is initially not connected to the
mother-of-bye-bye; the self-of-nursing is not the same self as the
self-of-cuddling-with-daddy. In psychoanalytic terms, self and
other are part-selves and part-objects.

Initially, too, I-schemes are mind–body units (in Piaget's [see
Gruber and Voneche, 1977] terms, sensorimotor schemes). In its
nursing activity, the infant does not distinguish its thinking,
feeling, and perceiving from its bodily sensations and actions.
As long as the mental and physical aspects of the baby's self
world engagements are not differentiated, no thought can occur
that is not also being enacted motorically, no emotion without
its bodily concomitants. The early I-self, therefore, is profoundly
a body self. It is not a body self in the sense Freud (1911)
hypothesized, in which the infant is oblivious to the world outside of its own body. Rather, the infant's ways of going about
things in its world are bodily ways, and its thought and affect
patterns are patterns of bodily action.

I-schemes are the patterns (templates) by which infants understand and act in their worlds. Most immediately, the nursing
scheme at a given moment patterns the baby's actions in subsequent nursing events and is modified in various ways by them. In
an infant's application of this template to events outside nursing,
we might see a three-month old widely open her mouth in enthu-
siastic welcome of her grandmother. In psychoanalytic terms, it is
her "oral" way of saying hello. For Kernberg's (1966) patient,
rejected-depreciated-little-boy-with-harsh-and-haughty-adult
was one pattern by which he understood an interchange with
someone else; longing-guilt-ridden-child-with-all-forgiving-all-
loving-grown-up was another.

Stern (1994) movingly details ways in which infants whose

mothers are depressed might establish particular templates or protonarrative envelopes that pattern their ways of being with others, both in infancy and later life. Mothers who are depressed tend to break eye contact and do not easily respond to their infants' overtures. In their fluctuating mood states, they are variously more and less available to their children. Intense efforts to meet their children's needs for stimulation may lead them to go through the motions of responsiveness though unable to muster the relevant feelings. Infants, then, might establish various schemes of "being-with" (Stern's term), rooted in their efforts to reanimate their "dead" mothers. They might establish interaction patterns persisting into adulthood in identifications with their depressed mothers, in fears that engagement might at any moment eventuate in loss or abandonment, or in other templates specific to particular infant–mother dyads.

I-Self Development by Integration and Differentiation

I-self development, beyond this form of scheme modification in successive enactments of the same scheme, occurs by the integration of the discrete I-schemes and differentiation within them. It occurs by processes Winnicott (1971) and Piaget (Flavell, 1963) describe in strikingly similar ways. Both Winnicott and Piaget posit interaction modes consonant with I-schemes as fundamental to development. In both Winnicott's and Piaget's models, the infant initially defines the persons and objects of activities in terms of the schemes of which they are a part. In Winnicott's example, the mother of an affectively positive event is not the same mother for the infant as the mother of an affectively negative one. The infant self is a good self in the first, a bad self in the second. In Piaget's example, the infant defines a ring differently when it is part of a grasping activity than when it is the object of visual tracking: it is only a "graspable" in the first, and no more than a "seeable" in the second. Implicit in Piaget's conception, the infant self-of-grasping is not the same self for the baby as the self-of-visual-tracking.

Winnicott and Piaget provide virtually identical descriptions of integration and differentiation processes occurring in babies' development at about three to four months of age. Winnicott's example focuses on the integration of affectively positive and negative interaction modes in the "holding situation"; Piaget's speaks to the infant's integration of its visual tracking and grasp schemes in its dealings with a ring.[4] Both Winnicott and Piaget propose that development occurs when the infant activates two disparate interaction modes in relation to the same object. In Winnicott's example, when the mother comfortably holds the distressed infant, the baby activates both its good-mother–good-self scheme and its bad-mother–bad-self scheme in relation to her. In Piaget's, when the baby tries to grasp the ring it is tracking visually, it is activating both its vision and its grasp schemes toward the ring.

The results are momentous. When the infant enacts two disparate schemes toward the same object (the mother, the ring) the two dynamic schemes are integrated with one another. In Winnicott's example, when the infant integrates its negative and positive feelings toward its mother, they are modulated by one another, and, as the process continues, the child becomes increasingly capable of ambivalence, in which it holds both positive and negative feelings toward another simultaneously. In Piaget's example, when the infant integrates its vision and grasp schemes, it becomes flexibly able to use looking and grasping together in its engagements with its environment.

In both paradigms, this integration of schemes also results in

---

[4] In Piaget's view, visual tracking and grasping are distinct action modalities represented mentally in sensorimotor schemes. He uses the integration of these schemes as a paradigmatic example of psychic integration generally. Currently a significant body of research (Rose and Russ, 1987) suggests that originally these modalities may be undifferentiated rather than discrete: the infant responds to an object without distinguishing whether it is seeing or grasping it. Development, then, occurs by the differentiation of the two modes rather than by their integration. If that view should prevail as the evidence mounts, Piaget's conception might have to be taken in more metaphoric terms than the literal ones in which he proposed it.

differentiations of self and nonself within them: the infant begins to differentiate its contribution to an interaction from that of the nonself. In Winnicott's conception, the infant begins to become aware of the mother's feelings as distinct from its own. In Piaget's, as children become increasingly able to differentiate their own parts in interactions from those of others and the impersonal world, they become more and more able to distinguish their own actions from causal forces and to locate themselves within general space and time frames distinct from themselves.

Every instance of integration–differentiation, moreover, contributes, in both Winnicott's and Piaget's conceptions, to the differentiation of the mental from the bodily aspects of schemes. When the infant of Winnicott's example integrates its feelings of comfort and discomfort, the bodily aspects of neither its comfortable interaction with its mother nor its uncomfortable interactions can fully be a part of the new, modulated feeling. To that small extent, the infant's feelings are becoming free of their bodily concomitants. When Piaget's infant grasps the ring it sees, the bodily components of grasping and seeing are modified in the integration of the two schemes. Both grasping and seeing are now a little less absolutely tied to particular bodily activations. In the subsequent myriad integrations and differentiations of development, both become so free of particular physical activations that they can be activated entirely in the mind. The capacity for the "trial action" that in Freud's view signals the transition from id to ego (from non-*Ich* to *Ich* ways of undestanding events) is being established.

Winnicott did not focus explicitly on the child's growing sense of I-ness in the context of these processes. In Piaget's view, which is accepted here, a sense of I-ness depends on the extent to which the integration and differentiation of schemes have proceeded (see Flavell, 1963). In later life we might see, as in Loewald's (1980) example, that as a woman integrates her feelings toward her husband and father into the network of motivations that constitutes her self, her experience of a "compulsion" that "plagues" her changes into a constellation of I-feelings. In

Ogden's (1986) illustrations, similarly, it is the integration of previously isolated wishes and feelings with the larger body of
one's experience that transforms a person's sense of an anxiety
"attack" or irresistible "need" to binge into an experience that
carries a personal sense of I-ness.

In the same processes, the infant begins to establish integrated and differentiated self and object representations. In
Winnicott's view, when the infant integrates its two ways of
interacting, it has made a beginning move toward an integrated
view of the mother as good–bad and of a good–bad self. In that
process, he suggests, the infant also begins to establish itself as
independent of its mother. Piaget delineates somewhat more
fully the processes by which increasingly differentiated and
integrated representations are established. In Piaget's view,
when the infant activates both schemes in relation to the ring,
the ring—a graspable in one scheme and a seeable in the
other—becomes a seeable-graspable and moves to this extent
toward becoming a whole object. Now, defined by both schemes,
it can no longer be a wholly undifferentiated aspect of either. To
this small extent it has become a representation independent of
any single scheme. It is beginning to become a permanent
object, permanent in the sense that it can occur mentally in the
absence of the actual object and its definition for the individual
does not change with every shift in desire, fear, or other dynamic
influence. The infant self, similarly, no more a grasper in one
scheme and a seer in the other, becomes a seer-grasper and
begins the long journey from a constellation of part-selves specific to each of a host of disparate interaction modes toward the
establishment of an integrated, whole self.

Both Winnicott and Piaget offer these paradigmatic examples
to illustrate processes fundamental to development and change
in our psychic structures throughout life. In all our lives, our I-
selves and me-selves develop together by processes of integration and differentiation. We integrate our I-schemes into larger
wholes and differentiate self from not-self within them when we
activate two disparate schemes in relation to the same person or
object. In these processes we establish and change the dynamic

constellations of our minds. If Kernberg's (1966) patient, for example, could experience both his rejected-self-with-haughty-adult I-self component and his loved-self-with-perfect-all-giving adult together toward Kernberg, the two I-scheme constellations might be modulated by one another toward more realistic and flexible patterns (templates) available to him in his interactions with Kernberg and with others in his life.

Every integration and differentiation of I-schemes also results in the establishment of self and object representatons. The individual is establishing an increasingly integrated me-self and a representational world distinct from self. The processes in which self (and object) representations are formed result in an intimate relationship between the me-self and the I-self. Every (initially inchoate) self (and object) representation is defined by the dynamic scheme in which it occurs. With every dynamic integration, representations are defined by larger numbers of schemes. At any moment, people's self representations (the me-self) reflect exactly the dynamic schemes then in play (the I-self).

This, in outline, is one view of how we might think about the I-self as composed of our ways of interacting with our worlds and about its relation to the me-self. It suggests one way of construing the basic units of interaction, their development by integration and differentiation, and their continuing relationships to self representations. The rest of this chapter deals with some of its theoretical implications in relatively broad terms and, with the help of a hypothetical clinical incident, some of its clinical ones, to prepare us for considerations of more specific issues in subsequent discussions.

The I-Self: A Constellation of Interactions?

It is perhaps not difficult to accept the idea that our I-selves are our ways of going about things. And, when we observe a person acting suspiciously toward another or like a depreciated child toward a haughty adult, we may easily accept these as personally motivated activities. But the bald assertion that our I-selves are made up of patterns of interaction may bring us up short. In our common view, interactions occur between self and other. How, then, can the self be a structure of interactions?

Our difficulty has historical roots. Since the Enlightenment, when the question of our relations to the world around us became newly important, Western thought has identified our sense organs as fundamental to our ways of knowing the world. Knowledge, and in particular scientific knowledge, must be based solidly on sensory data, enhanced, perhaps, by microscopes, refined measurement techniques, and so forth.

This view is central, too, to Freud's theory and, interestingly, to major object relations paradigms that have diverged from it. For Freud, sensory impressions of objects and events, accurately registered in the mind, are fundamental to psychic structure. Individual variations in experience and psychopathology occur when these representations are distorted by the drives. In that view, the function of psychoanalysis is to remove the drive distortions from representations and give individuals back the true (perception-based) histories of their lives.

Object relations perspectives developed in opposition to this view. Clinicians increasingly rejected the notion of isolated individuals with sense-based connections to the world. In their theory revisions, they proposed that people's self world connections occur in their active engagements with others. Even with this end in view, however, the powerful notion that sense-based representations are fundamental to our psychic structures prevailed.

In major object relational themes, basic interaction patterns are identified as self–other units, representations of self and other variously joined together or differentiated. The interaction itself, the perceptive-affective-cognitive interchange with the other, is present only implicitly, in the hyphen. The merger and differentiation of self and other, their integration into whole selves and whole objects, and their various patternings and pathological distortions are the substance of extensive and clinically valuable theoretical elaboration. But representations are not ways of relating, and, from the first, construing relationships not as engagements with our worlds but as self–other units has created major obstacles to clinical observation and conceptual formulation.[5]

The difficulties become particularly clear in considerations of the self aspects of self–other units. The notion that the object aspect of interactions is an object representation is generally accepted. But the self aspect has not found a satisfactory definition. It is typically defined as a perception-based representation coordinate to an object representation. This definition is widely accepted as sound conceptually, but it does not adequately accommodate the self aspects of interactions in clinical exploration.

When self aspects of interactions are explored clinically, people are seen to be active in their engagements with others: they are motivated toward contact with them; they understand their relations to others in various ways; they love or hate or envy others; in optimum development they establish sophisticated intersubjective relations with them. These are clearly engagements with others in self–other relationships. But the self involved in these engagements cannot be the self aspect of a self–other unit. As typically defined, that self is a self representation coordinate to an object representaton. But a representation cannot be motivated toward objects, love or hate them, or have intersubjective relationships with them. No widely accepted

---

[5] Kernberg's (1966) seminal, if flawed, proposal illustrates the heavy pressure against a more direct focus on the interaction itself. He proposes more than a hyphen to join self and other. Affects are the link between them in his conception. He intends a model of affective interactions that reflects his clinical obervations. In his formal conception, however, he cannot get away from the notion of perception-based self and object representations as fundamental and of impersonal drive forces acting on them. The resulting construct, that interaction units are self and object representations linked by affect derivatives of impersonal drives, is not one that easily lends itself to exploring people's ways of relating to others.

notion of self that includes both its place coordinate to object representations and its activity in interaction with others has been found in the framework based on self–other units. Jacobson's (1964) sensitive and complex explorations of the place of self in an object relations perspective illuminates problems in doing so and the difficulty of their resolution.

These difficulties are not at all surprising. It is axiomatic in this culture that sensory inputs are basic to experience and psychic structure. To posit interactions rather than sense perceptions as fundamental is more radical than may easily be recognized. It has the whole weight of the culture against it. In academic psychology Piaget has most thoroughly elaborated this perspective. Within psychoanalytic psychology it has been most fully explored by Loewald (1980) and Ogden (1986). In both Piagetian psychology (espectially as elaborated by Kegan, 1982) and the psychoanalytic perspectives, these interactions are personally motivated engagements with the world. In both they are identified with the I-self.

The focus on interactions rather than sensory impressions as the basic units of experience and mental representation offers one solution to the conceptual quandaries posed by the self–other unit. The unit of relationship is now a dynamic scheme of personally motivated interaction rather than a pair of representations joined by a hyphen. Self is not one constituent of a pair of representations; it is both the individual's personal ways of interacting with others (the I-self) and the self representations that emerge from them (the me-self).

There is, of course, a major sense in which I-schemes can properly be thought of as self–other units. They represent actual interactions between self and other. Although schemes are initially global, without differentiation of their self and nonself aspects, the establishment of a distinct self and other within them is a major developmental accomplishment.

Even then, however, the self and other aspects of schemes are more than representations. Each has both representational and dynamic aspects. In the course of self–other differentiation, we do establish distinct representations of the self and other interactions. But that is not all. We also differentiate the dynamic aspects of schemes: we attribute some perceptive-cognitive-affective aspects of interactions to ourselves, others to the other interaction participant. The differentiation outcomes are people's personal ways of perceiving, thinking, and feeling coordinate to those they attribute to others, and the representations of self and other that stand for these dynamic constellations.[6]

Moreover, the interaction mode is not a hyphen that disappears as the individual differentiates self and other. On the contrary, our ways of interacting are fundamental. They constitute our I-selves. We differentiate self and other *within* them (the self and mother as aspects of the comfortable-holding scheme; the depreciated child and haughty adult of the patient's transference scheme). Throughout our lives our interaction schemes, their self and other aspects differentiated to varying extents, are the templates by which we encode our experience. They pattern our ways of understanding and acting in our worlds.

But What of the Me-Self, Our self Representations?

The me-self, in this view, is not a sensory registration modified by drives. Dynamic functions, our interaction schemes, are primary. Representations or images emerge from them, and throughout our lives our representations whether of self or objects, realistic or unrealistic, are defined by, and stand for, the constellation of interaction schemes then in play.

---

[6] This concept opens the way for new explorations of "objects." Benjamin's (1988, 1995) understanding of intersubjectivity is particularly useful in this area. The I-self model suggests that, in the course of development, we establish increasingly differentiated and integrated notions of our own and others' parts in interactions. It is in these integration–differentiation processes that we become increasingly sophisticated intersubjective beings.

For a youngster, depending on the I-schemes then active, a ring might be the graspable of Piaget's example or perhaps a circle for ring-around-the-rosie, a hoop, a halo around the moon, or a marriage signifier. For a 10-year-old girl, depending on fluctuations of mood, current relationship configurations, or particular conflict, her mother may be, for her, not only the good or bad mother of Winnicott's example, but a tease, a deadly competitor, or the best of friends. A man in the throes of grief might at different moments view himself as utterly desolate, a playboy suddenly free, a zombie dead to all that is good, or a computer brain with no need for sentiment.

In important ways this view of images or representations and their relation to dynamic forces matches Freud's clinically near conceptions. In Freud's view of dreams and symptoms, every image or representation stands for the dynamic forces active at the time. Every dream image is constructed by an underlying constellation of wishes, envies, loves, conflicts, and defenses. Every hysterical paralysis, stomach pain, or facial tic stands for a body of personal motivations.

In Freud's view, however, representations are structured by dynamic forces only in abnormal circumstances. They are unrealistic, subjective rather than objective. Our representations of trees, of other persons, of a rocker, or of a mother's arm are not structured in that way. They are perception-based registrations in the mind. They are our connections to the real world and, in Freud's view, to objective reality. Only when the ordinary processes of perception are overwhelmed by the drives, as in the case of symptoms, or held in abeyance by sleep, as in the case of dreams, are representations structured by dynamic forces.[7]

But, if we argue that *all* representatons are constructed by, and stand for, dynamic schemes, must we give up all possibil-

---

[7] The problems inherent in this view have been particularly obvious in considerations of self representations. While it might seem at least superficially acceptable to consider that an object representation is based on perceptual representations of that object, it has been virtually impossible to accept that our self representations reflect sense perceptions of ourselves subsequently modified by drives.

ity of objectivity? In some meanings of that word, yes. Johnson (1987) provides us with a succinct overview of our commonly held, and in his view untenable, notions of objectivism:

> The world consists of objects that have properties and stand in various relationships independent of human understanding. The world is as it is, no matter what any person happens to believe about it, and there is one correct "God's-Eye-View" about what the world really is like. In other words, there is a rational structure to reality independent of the beliefs of any particular people, and correct reason mirrors this rational structure [p. x].

In this construction of objectivity, the representations of Freud's conception are objective; representations as construed here are not. In the proposed view, subjectivity pervades all experience: I-schemes, our ways of understanding the world, are fundamental to our construction of representations. Our representations of self and nonself do not correspond directly with the objects of the actual world; they correspond to the constellation of interaction schemes active at the moment. Their meanings are not objective or rational in the sense that they consist only in their relations to things in the world, independent of the beliefs and purposes of any particular people; rather, their meanings depend fundamentally on our beliefs and purposes.

Does it follow, then, that any representation is as valid as any other? If our ways of understanding the world are not rational structures that mirror the rational structure of reality, must we give up the notion that we have connections with the world that make one representation more realistic than another? Not at all. Our connections with the world do not occur by the sensory perception of objects or a uniquely human capacity for rationality that mirrors the rational structure of the world. They occur in our interactions with the world.[8]

---

[8] Loewald (1976) describes the interaction of internal schemata and environmental events in perception with particular clarity as to its implications for psychoanalytic theory and practice.

In its interactions, the infant continually discovers and revises its notions about the environment's parameters. Its nursing scheme, for example, is modified in successive nursing incidents to take into account with increasing accuracy such real-world matters as the mother's movements, the motion and sound of the rocker, its own nursing rhythms. Every success and failure in its interactions tells the infant directly about the adequacy of its notions of the world (it grasps, or fails to grasp, the breast or bottle). Every accommodation of an action that leads to greater success reflects increased accuracy in the baby's sense of the way the world works. In psychoanalytic terms, reality testing occurs from the beginning in infants' interactions with their worlds.

The matter becomes more complicated when the child, at about age two, becomes able to act mentally without motor enactment. Now, when the child can imagine actions to be taken in the future (a trip to grandma tomorrow) or actions that cannot occur at all in the real world (flying with Peter Pan), actions can no longer be validated directly and immediately by their success or failure. More complicated reality tests must be constructed that include matters of convention (what may and may not be called a dog), of social appropriateness (the new sibling may not be returned to the store), and of increased cognitive complexity (the class of flying beings does not include people).

In the course of our lives, then, our me-selves, our representations of self (like our object representations), are shaped by our interactions with the human and nonhuman world. To varying degrees we test them against reality in the broad sense just outlined. Throughout life our me-selves (like all representations) stand for the constellations of I-schemes active in the moment. They may vary from the altogether stable to the most evanescent. In ordinarily successful development, we tend to achieve a stable sense of ourselves as human, as gender specific, perhaps as confident in our ability to meet the vicissitudes of life. In tending a new baby, we might reevoke, for a moment, remembered me-self representations of being safe, of smelling baby powder, or of being cuddled. In hopeful anticipation of the future, we might elaborate me-self representations as a career success, or, in anticipatory dread, representations of ourselves as old and infirm. In dreams or daydreams, we may construct fleeting me-self representations of ourselves in flight over the city or as ruler of Monaco.

An Unacceptable Anthropomorphism?

These conceptions of the I-self and the me-self do not meet Hartmann's requirement that a rigorous examination of mental life must be framed in terms of impersonal forces. Hartmann and his colleagues (1942) agree with widely voiced criticisms that the structural concepts of psychoanalysis are often used in inappropriately metaphoric terms, as if the id, the ego, and the superego were persons in various relations to one another.

Hartmann et al. acknowledged that anthropomorphic metaphors might justifiably be used to delineate observed processes when a fully developed theory has not yet been achieved. They cite Freud's familiar observation, "The Ego presented itself to the Superego as love object," and suggest that this mode of expression is helpful clinically. Under certain conditions, superego approval of the self might be a kind of self love that substitutes for loving another person. The use of metaphor here is justifiable, in Hartmann et al.'s view, because we do not yet have more scientifically acceptable frameworks that can accommodate these insights.

They emphasize, however, that metaphor must not substitute for theory. A more rigorous description of this circumstance would not speak of "approval" or "disapproval" by the superego but simply "of different kinds and degrees of tension between two psychic organizations, according to the presence or absence of conflict between their functions. Approval would be characterized by a diminution of tension; disapproval by its increase" (p. 16).

The argument that the id, ego, and superego cannot properly be discussed as if they were human beings is easy to accept; no case has been made that the characteristics of persons can be mapped in any useful way onto those of the id, ego, and super-ego. Curiously enough, though, Hartmann and his colleagues did not address the question of anthropomorphism in a more apposite arena, that is, in relation to the wishes, aims, fears, con-flicts, and defenses that make up the id, ego, and superego. They seem to have accepted unquestioningly that these must be con-sidered to be impersonal forces. But these are the very processes that Freud described as I-activities (*das Ich, das Ueberich,* and, less certainly, *das Es*). They are the constituents of the I-self.

Must we consider explorations of the I-self as beyond the scope of science? Is it necessary, perhaps, to turn to the humani-ties with their quite different criteria for the study of its parame-ters? I think not. The conceptions underlying I-schemes are not foreign to bodies of research widely accepted in psychology, most familiarly those based on Piaget's work. The organization of I-schemes, the processes of their development, and their rela-tions to the me-self are fully in accord with Piaget's ideas. Extensive theoretical and empirical investigations of Piaget's conceptions have not found them to be inappropriately anthro-pomorphic. It appears valid to argue, then, that a focus on personally motivated interaction schemes rather than on imper-sonal forces need not by itself exclude a conception from objec-tive examination. Inappropriate anthropomophism need not be feared. In fact, if people's ways of interacting are actually per-sonally motivated, studies of them as if they were not are likely to be of limited usefulness.

A Clinical Illustration

The following hypothetical clinical interchange suggests some of the ways the notions elaborated here might illumi-nate the familiar processes of a clinical hour differently from those that posit representations modified by impersonal forces as primary.

Let us say that a young man begins a clinical hour with his therapist with excited praise for his partner's clever business maneuver and follows it with a smiling aside about the same man's apparent inability to keep his shoes tied and his tie straight. Soon he remembers an adolescent friend, an envied lady-killer, who, curiously enough, has not made good in the real (business) world. As the hour proceeds, it occurs to him that an observation the therapist made in the previous hour turned out to be right on the mark. Within a few moments, though, he notes that the therapist's plant seems to be dying.

In the course of the hour, the therapist becomes increasingly aware of the pattern of idealization and half-hidden contempt in the patient's relationships to his partner, his remembered friend, and herself. This is a commonplace of clinical work. The therapist's listening ear does not typically center on the object representations of such a series of associations, but on the relationships the patient expresses and reexpresses in them. The clinical aim is not a search for a veridical object representation disguised in a series of drive-determined displacements to the partner, the friend, and the therapist, but an exploration of the affective-cognitive interaction modes common to his engagements with them.

As the patient talks of these matters, the therapist notes that he is quite childlike in his awe struck admiration of his partner but is righteously superior in his demeanor when he notes his partner's grooming failures. Similarly, his tone and word choice are boyish as he speaks of his sexually sophisticated friend of adolescence but is crisply businesslike when he rejects him as an economic failure. And his subtle scorn for the therapist's inadequacy as a grower of plants contrasts with his almost giddy praise of her insightful observation.

In pursuing these observations, a commitment to representations as fundamental invites attention to distortions in the patient's object representations and the drives reflected in the patterning of his idealization and scorn. A focus on the patient's ways of interacting with his world highlights the possibility that his associations reflect two discrete interaction modes, two templates or codes by which he understands his engagements with others. In one he stands in awe struck admiration of the other; in the other, he feels contemptuous, scornful, and rejecting of that person.

Like Kernberg's (1966) patient, this hypothetical one expresses these disparate interaction modes discretely, as if they were two selves completely separated from one another. The self and other of the two interaction modes are part-selves and part-objects. The self is an awed naive child in the first and, in the second, a superior, critical business success. The other of the first interaction mode is awe inspiring, clever, and sophisticated and, in the second, a poorly groomed, economically and horticulturally inadequate inferior.

Let us suppose that the therapist draws attention to the idealization–scorn contrast and that the patient is able actively to experience his two conflicting interaction modes together quite directly, as he feels them toward his therapist. A focus on drive distortions of initially accurate representations invites attention to the more veridical perception of the therapist that might result from the patient's experiencing her in both idealizing and demeaning terms and to the modulation of the patient's idealizing and scorning drive derivatives by one another.

Highlighting interactions as central suggests a broad range of clinically familiar outcomes. As the patient expresses these contrary I-schemes toward the therapist, he integrates his idealizing and scorning ways of going at things. They become modulated by one another and more flexibly available to him in his dealings with other persons, such as his colleague, and, in memory, his friend of adolescence. In that integration process his I-schemes also become more differentiated. He more accurately ascribes aspects of these interactions to himself and to the therapist; perhaps he comes to the realization that he and she both contributed to the processes that enabled her to make the insightful observation that he so admired (but, in another context, might have utterly disparaged). It is in these dynamic integrations and differentiations, too, that he achieves a more vivid sense of his feelings and actions as his own, as I-activities.

Changes in his representations of himself and the therapist exactly reflect the dynamic changes he has achieved. His disparate senses of himself as naive child and superior critic give way to a more realistic representation of his unique adult self, capable of both criticism and admiration; his representation of his therapist now more fully includes her competencies and her imperfections, and his sense of her as distinct from himself is enlarged. To the extent that his two ways of going about things are modified in a lasting way, his representations of self and other will also be modified as they occur in relation to his colleague and his remembered friend. More broadly, his integration of these two I-schemes will affect the ways he views himself and others in situations at other times and in other places in which he activates them. It is always, in this view, our I-schemes that structure our self (and other) representations.

Summary

This chapter has presented one model for a notion of the I-self (the dynamic self) and its relations to the me-self (self representations). It posits personally motivated schemes of interaction (I-schemes), rather than sense impressions modified by drives, as the basic structures of the mind. These I-schemes constitute our I-selves, our ways of going about things. The me-self, our self representations, emerges from I-schemes. Throughout our lives our self representations, are defined by the constellation of I-schemes active in the moment and, in turn, are shaped by the I-schemes of the past.

Initially our personally motivated interactions with our worlds are registered in undifferentiated, discrete sensorimotor schemes of perceptual-cognitive-affective-physical self–world activity. Change, whether as a result of development or therapy, occurs through the integration and differentiation of these I-schemes. It occurs when a person, at whatever stage in life, activates two disparate interaction modes toward the same object. Then the person's two distinct ways of perceiving, thinking, and feeling (perhaps early positive and negative infant–mother interactions, or idealizing and scornful ones of later clinical work) are modulated by one another. Their self and nonself aspects are more differentially ascribed to the self and nonself. Self and nonself are integrated across I-schemes to form more complexly whole-selves and whole-objects. The initially absolute tie of the mental to the physical-motoric is loosened and gradually permits action to occur in the mind with or without its physical-motoric concomitants. It is in the course of these integration–differentiation processes that people achieve an increasing sense of I-ness in their activities. Concurrently, in ways that precisely match these dynamic changes, the self and object representations of the two ways of interacting are integrated and differentiated.

Throughout our lives, our I-selves are the codes or templates by which we understand and act in our worlds. Both in early development and in later life our I-schemes are to varying degrees integrated and differentiated. The varied patterns that result and their consequences provide the material of future chapters.

In the next chapter, we will focus on contributions from various areas of investigation to our ways of construing the templates we identify with the I-self. Some have structured areas of psychoanalytic thinking almost from its inception. Others are currently emerging from such diverse fields as philosophy, linguistics, the humanities, and academic psychology. They explore our ways of making meaning, the ways we understand and act in our worlds. They offer ways to refine and expand our notions of how we might construe our ways of interacting as our I-selves.

3 THE I-SELF: OUR WAYS OF MAKING MEANING

If we argue that our I-selves are our ways of going about things, patterning our perceptions, understanding events, and acting in our lives, we find ourselves in the middle of a major controversy about whether we *discover* meaning or *construct* it. The I-self perspective comes down on the side of constructivism.

Moreover, in this view our meaning-making structures take a particular form: they are the I-schemes that constitute our dynamic selves. These I-schemes are dynamic schemes of personally motivated interactions. They differ developmentally and in adult life in the degree to which they are integrated with one another, the degree to which their self and nonself aspects are differentiated, and the extent to which they can be activated mentally without their bodily components. Their personally motivated character qualifies them as I-schemes, but they differ widely in the degree to which people experience their expression as I-activities. They develop in processes of integration and differentiation. Together with the self representations that emerge from them, I-schemes form the dynamic and representational aspects of the self: the I-self and the me-self.

Currently, discussions about what it might mean to say that we construct meaning rather than discover it and about how we might imagine our meaning making structures are proliferating in a wide range of academic and clinical disciplines. To suggest that we make meaning and that our I-selves are the organizations by which we do so invites comparison with other constructivist frameworks that have been proposed in the past and that are currently emerging. In this chapter we explore ways in which the notion that I-schemes are the structures by which we understand and act in our worlds might converge with others within psychoanalytic psychology and outside it.

Libidinal Patterns of Meaning Making

It is one of Freud's most spectacular and lasting contributions to have shown that people make meaning of their experiences in configurations established in their earliest childhoods. Almost from the beginning, he saw that his patients' associations about their lives and their sufferings fell into patterns that they repeated again and again in their life activities: in dealing with possessions, handling issues of food and money, engaging in particular interests and ideas, or making love. With elegant simplicity, Freud argued that people establish these constellations very early in their lives, in the course of their feeding and toileting experiences, or in resolving issues of the differences between the sexes and the oedipal conflicts that follow. I can remember the indignation in my own professional community that greeted his suggestion that the complex and often deplorable ways people behave in adulthood can be traced to their experiences in the (putative) innocence of childhood. Its wider emotional resonance is suggested in the fervor with which it was accepted in psychoanalytic circles and, as Douglas (1995) details in her remarkable evocation of New York in the 20s, in the broader reaches of society.

Freud himself concentrated intensively on tracing his patients' ways of understanding their experience and acting in their worlds to constellations developed in their early lives. In his case study of the young Russian nobleman known as the Wolf Man, for example, Freud (1918) showed how the patient's utter refusal to accept the idea that, being male, he could not bear children patterned his childhood phobia, his early cruelty to small animals, his later religious preoccupations, and his ferocious arguments in adulthood with his mother and sister over money.

Abraham (1921) extended Freud's explorations with his fine eye for clinical observation. In his view, the developmentally early patterns by which people interpret their experience give rise to their character traits. A patient's statement, for example, that "everything that is not me is dirt" seemed to Abraham to point directly to the patient's traits of pretentiousness and arrogance and to their developmental roots in his toileting experiences. It struck Abraham, too, that apparently unconnected character aspects might be expressions of a single developmental constellation. People who have a strong yearning to "obtain everything," for example, might also have an obstinate urge to talk. They feel themselves to be overflowing with ideas and believe that what they have to say has a special power or unusual value. Both of these quite disparate character traits, he suggests, might be expressions of a single constellaton in which patients play out the mother–child feeding relationship—both the infant's longing to "obtain everything" and, in the urge to talk, the mother's unbounded giving.

The characteristics of these constellations seem to echo the patterns of meaning making we identify as the I-self. To call them "patterns" might suggest impersonal maps or frames that govern people's ways of understanding events. That was not at all

Freud's view. The patterns he observed express personal urgencies: the ways a boy might feel compelled toward being cruel to animals, the arrogance of a man who sees others as dirt, or a person's stubborn determination to speak, whatever the situation. They are expressed in interactions, in individuals' engagements with other people or the nonhuman world. More than this, Abraham seems to suggest that they originate in, and are structured by, early interactions, most inescapably perhaps, in his observation that a person's character traits might reflect both his own and his mother's parts in the nursing situation of infancy.

In Freud's formal theory, however, these ways of making meaning reflect only meaning making that has been distorted by drives. Fundamentally, the meanings of objects and events are registered accurately in the mind. The ways of making meaning that become central to psychoanalytic exploration are formed when these veridical, sense-based representations are distorted by drives, in the foregoing cases by libidinal ones. In the theory, though not in the clinical observations, the place of the self remains ambiguous. In Freud's (1918) clinical explorations of the Wolf Man's difficulties in living, he unambiguously treats his patient's urges toward cruelty, his religious ruminations about the virgin birth, and his ferocity toward his mother and sister as personally motivated. They are *Ich* activities. Abraham (1921), too, seems quite clearly to imply that a person's arrogance or his driven urge to talk is an I-activity. The libido theory, however, takes little note of self. It speaks to instinct-based drives and objects. We are not selving when we are making meaning. Our ways of understanding our experiences are not I-activities; they are patterns structured by drive cathexes of objects.

Meaning Making Is Agentic

Schafer (1976) proposes a view of our ways of making meaning that accommodates Freud's and Abraham's (1921) clinical observations and moves toward establishing a theoretical framework that more fully accommodates them. He moves away from the objectivist framework underlying Freud's conception that ways of making meaning rooted in our early experiences are drive distortions of our accurate sense-based views of the world. Instead, he argues that the meanings of objects and events are not originally given in nature at all: we *make* meaning, not only as distortions of veridical sensory input but in all our perceptions, cognitions, memories, fantasies, and anticipations. All our ways of constructing meaning are personally motivated. No object or event occurs in the mind devoid of the personal agentic activity by which we construct its meaning.

Different people may construct their experiences of the same event differently, each for reasons of his or her own. Many of these reasons originate in early life and persist unconsciously as primitive forms of emotional and cognitive experience. The Wolf Man's arguments with his mother and sister were, in this view, not products of impersonal drives, the libidinal distortion of veridically registered experience. They resulted from his personal ways of making meaning, rooted in his early conflicts about the differences between the sexes.

Schafer identifies these agentic ways of making meaning as I-activities. He prefers, however, not to think of them as self actions, for the term self seems to him to have too many and contradictory meanings to be useful. Rather, he suggests that we think of the person or subject, rather than the self, as making meaning.

But that proposal has its own difficulties. The "person" or "subject" has no defined place in psychoanalytic psychology. Moreover, the notion that it is the person who makes meaning shares the difficulties that James (1892) ascribed to the notion of the I-self as a person or agent that acts in certain ways: if the I-self is found not in the meaning-making processes themselves but in the "person," we are faced with the conceptual problem of showing how this "person" is to be construed in psychoanalytic theory generally and, specifically, what it might mean to say that this "person" constructs meaning.

Meaning Making Is Interpersonal

Like Schafer, Loewald (1980) fully accepts the notion that we construct all our meanings and that we do so in personally motivated ways. He adds an interpersonal dimension. He proposes, congruently with the I-self view, that the personally motivated patterns by which we understand our experience are relational patterns.

Loewald argues, like Schafer, that perceptions, facts, and events are not given in nature. They are products of our interpretation. All these interpretations, the meanings we ascribe to events, are personally motivated. Unlike Schafer, however, Loewald views our ways of making meaning as self activities, though, as noted earlier, he reserves the term self for those interpretations we arrive at consciously (with a sense of I-ness).

Loewald's conception of how these relational structures develop converges in major ways with the I-self model. In his view, the structures of the mind are at base personally motivated forces patterned in infant–mother interactions. All development occurs in active processes of meaning making that result in increasingly integrated and differentiated networks of interaction schemata. These networks pattern the ways we interact with our worlds and, in turn, are continuously modified as we interact with our worlds in new ways.

Loewald's perspective accommodates, and suggests refinements of, Abraham's (1921) observations of the man who both wants to obtain everything and stubbornly insists on talking. His views, and the ones proposed here, invite us to notice that Abraham's interpretation of his observations, extraordinary for its time, requires some modification in an interactional model of development. The man's character traits, as Abraham described them, cannot simply reflect the mother's and the child's parts in the nursing interaction as though they were objective facts accurately registered in the mind. Rather, the man, now in his adulthood, makes meaning of events in patterns that appear to express a child's incompletely differentiated sense of his own part and his mother's in their feeding relationship. In his wish to "obtain everything," he may express his infant yearning for utter fulfillment from his mother, but, in his urge to talk he expresses not a mother's own feelings about nursing but, perhaps, a youngster's infantile attributions to her. His readiness to talk at any moment may reflect an infant boy's sense of his mother's eagerness at any moment to feed him. It may be his own sense that she is overflowing with milk that he expresses in his feeling that he is bursting with things to say. His own feelings of the special value and power of his mother's milk inform his overvaluation of his verbal productions. In his child's view, her gift is given by mouth and he expresses it through talking, but, of course, although he receives the wonderful milk by mouth, the mother herself "gives" not with her mouth but with her breast.

In his considerations of meaning making, Loewald remains, as always, acutely sensitive to the clinical implications of his ideas. It seems to him that, although meaning making is central to all the activities of our minds, clinical psychoanalysis is a special case. In psychoanalysis, the making of meaning is not secondary to other goals; its *essence* is the making and remaking of meaning. In the course of the psychoanalytic work of interpretation, new meanings are constructed from everything that transpires psychically—dreams, slips of the tongue, symptoms, fantasies, thoughts, behavior, moods, emotions, memories, plans, actions, decisions, choices made or contemplated, physical illnesses, life circumstances. As we modify our ways of making meaning, we are modifying our inner worlds. We are changing our minds.

Meaning Making is Selving

Kegan (1982) most fully identifies meaning making with self: the doing that the self is, is the making of meaning. Like Schafer

(1976) and Loewald (1980), he argues that there is no feeling, no experience, no thought, no perception independent of a meaning-making context. Unlike Schafer, however, he does not posit a person who makes meaning. In terms only slightly different from Loewald's, he suggests, instead, that "the activity of being a person is the activity of meaning-making" (p. 11). We *are* the ways we construct meaning, in patterns derived from early experiences of feeding and toileting, of comfortable and distressed infant–mother interactions, of grasping and visual tracking, and of all our subsequent ways of interacting with our worlds as they are modulated in the course of experience.

The Intergenerational Making of Meaning

Can our ways of making meaning, originating in our own early lives, have transgenerational effects? Do they prefigure the ways our children will understand their own experiences? Research based on Bowlby's concept of attachment, and elaborated in the context of Ainsworth's Strange Situation and Main's Adult Attachment Interview, suggests powerfully and movingly that they do (Goldberg, Muir, and Kerr, 1995).

Bowlby proposed that, on the basis of repeated experiences of characteristic patterns of interaction, children establish an Internal Working Model. This working model embodies their expectations regarding the nature of interactions between themselves and others and comes to organize their behavior in all significant relationships. It is a code or template by which they understand and act in their interpersonal worlds. A large number of studies using Ainsworth's Strange Situation have shown that, by 12 months of age, children have established stable attachment patterns the effects of which can be observed well into the children's school years (Karen, 1994).

Main and her colleagues have extended these investigations

to explore children's working models of attachment as functions of their caregivers' accounts of their own childhood attachment and separation experiences. Using Main's Adult Attachment Interview as a way to assess caregivers' working models, investigators have been able to demonstrate, across numerous studies, strong relationships between caregivers' security of attachment patterns and those of their children.

Bowlby's conception of how these attachment patterns might be transmitted from parent to child has been widely accepted. He outlined a three-part process. First, the parent's attachment-related experiences in childhood are embodied in a working model; this model then patterns the caregiver's mental representation of the child; that mental representation, in turn, determines parenting functions that constitute the primary determinants of the child's quality of attachment to the parent.

Fonagy and his colleagues (1993), focusing on people's capacities for self reflection, have begun to explore variables that might intervene to modify this transmission. They have found that some parents, more than others, are self reflective in their accounts of their own childhoods in the attachment interviews. In their accounts, those parents refer to the limited power of wishes, thoughts, and desires with respect to the real world; they acknowledge the opaqueness of the mental world of the other; they recognize that other people have their own thoughts and feelings; they speak of the possibility of diverse perspectives on the same event.

In recent work, the investigators explored the contribution of mothers' self reflectiveness to their children's attachment patterns in families that had undergone significant stresses and deprivations of kinds associated with insecure attachment (father absence, overcrowding, paternal unemployment, life-threatening illness of father or mother, parental criminality, psychiatric illness of the parents, major illnesses in childhood). The results are striking. Of 10 mothers in the stressed group with high "reflective" self ratings, all 10 had children who were securely attached. Only 1 of 17 children of stressed mothers with low self reflection ratings was securely attached.

The notion that our ways of interacting with others are rooted in early interactions with caregivers is not new to psychoanalytic psychology. However, the construction of a measure that powerfully identifies patterns of interaction as early as the end of the first year of life and demonstrations that these patterns persist in later interactions with peers and teachers are major contributions. The growing evidence that the ways adults understand their own childhood attachment experiences pattern their ways of interacting with their own children extends these results intergenerationally.

In the work of these investigators, Bowlby's Internal Working Model is central. Working models are interaction structures by which we make meaning of our relationships. They arise from infants' personal engagements with their caregivers.

At this point in the ongoing research, internal working models are not seen to be dynamic. They more closely resemble plans or maps than the powerfully active functions of Freud's libidinally based patterns of meaning making, or those of Schafer (1976) and Loewald (1980). The processes by which working models develop in childhood and the ways they might change in the course of the life cycle are largely unelaborated: notions of integration and differentiation or other developmental or therapeutic processes that are typically seen to modify interaction structures have not yet become focal in the exploration of working models. Even the self reflective processes, in the view of Fonagy and his colleagues (1993), do not alter the parent's working model itself. Their function is only to make it possible for the parent to forestall its activation.

These may be issues for the future. In programs of empirical research, the choice of conceptual issues to be addressed depends heavily on the possibilities of finding ways to operationalize them. For now it may be enough to take pleasure in these investigators' exploring our ways of making meaning of our interactions with others as internal working models, and their inventive empirical demonstrations of how these meaning-making structures may influence our lives and those of our children.

Shapes of Meaning-Making Structures: Metaphors

In an astonishing confluence of ideas Lakoff, a linguist, and Johnson, a philosopher, (1980), have come together to propose conceptions of meaning making that are fundamentally different from those dominant in their disciplines. A common interest in metaphor brought them together. In their respective fields, metaphor is a topic of only marginal interest in the study of meaning. In the course of their work, however, they became convinced that of its central importance. Soon after beginning to collaborate on what they intended to be a brief paper, they discovered that raising the issues they wanted to address meant rejecting the objectivist assumptions of contemporary philosophy and linguistics that are taken for granted in the Western tradition. The aspect of objectivism centrally important here was the Cartesian gap it posits between our cognitive, conceptual, rational side and our bodily, perceptual, and emotional side. Meaning is aligned with the mental, rational dimension, whereas the bodily, imaginative, emotional side is of secondary importance. The latter introduces subjective elements that are irrelevant to the objective nature of true meaning.

In this framework, metaphor cannot be easily understood. Lakoff and Johnson became convinced that the understanding of metaphor, and, soon, the understanding of meaning in general, required that the idea of rational thought as primary, and body-based, imaginative experience as secondary, must be stood on its head. Human embodiment, with its subjective, imaginative, and emotional aspects, is *central* to our structures of understanding. It directly influences what and how things can be meaningful for us, the ways we are able to comprehend and reason about our experience, and the actions we take. Rational or propositional thought is not irrelevant to meaning making. It is, however, secondary rather than primary. It rests on a complex web of nonpropositional meaning structures that emerge from bodily experience.

In metaphoric thought, Lakoff and Johnson argue, we project patterns from one domain of experience to another in order to understand events in a domain of a different kind. Johnson (1987), in his subsequent work, argues that bodily experience is the fundamental domain from which we project to other, non-body contexts. For example, physical balancing is an activity we learn early in our lives. A baby stands, wobbles, and drops to the floor. It tries again and again and again until a new world opens up—the world of balanced erect posture. We come to know more about balance and imbalance in learning to balance on a bicycle, balancing objects in juggling, walking a fence rail.

In metaphoric projections of our bodily sense of balance, we might interpret the portrait of a face or even an abstract painting in terms of its balance. We speak of emotional balance or a balanced personality. In a rational argument, we might pile up evidence for our side, weigh the merits of one or another point, agree that two arguments carry equal weight, or feel the balance of an argument tip in our favor. In all these metaphoric projections, Johnson suggests, we experience a sense of spontaneity or aliveness that is rooted ultimately in the kinesthetic sense of body balance from which they spring.

In this view, the body-based oral and anal orientations at the heart of Freud's libidinal theory would be understood as meaning structures people have established in the feeding and toileting interactions of their early lives. In metaphoric projections of oral meaning structures to other contexts, they might understand a movie as something they "take in," interpret an angry person as "spitting" mad, find themselves "overflowing" with things to say, or feel that a concert has left them "satiated" by too rich a "diet" of music. Abraham's (1921) patient might be seen to have derived his meaning structure, "All that is not me is dirt," from his bodily toileting activities. In metaphoric projections to other contexts, we could imagine that he might understand being seated in a restaurant in ways that lead him to wipe his silver with pretentious care, interpret his bathroom activity in a friend's house in such a way that he arrogantly rejects the use of the bathroom fan.

Johnson (1987) proposes that our basic structures of understanding are schemas that fundamentally represent bodily activities. He refers to them as image schemata, but declares that they are by no means nondynamic maps or templates or mere passive receptacles into which experience is poured. In terms congruent with Loewald's (1980) and the I-schemes proposed in this book, they are dynamic patterns of personally motivated interaction by which people organize their experience and activities.

Unlike Freud, Johnson does not view these body-based ways of understanding our experience as distortions of true meanings or as necessarily private and idiosyncratic ways of interpreting our experience. Rather, in tune with Loewald's conception and that of I-schemes, he proposes that they underlie *all* our understandings. More than this, he finds in our body-based experience itself the shared meanings that Freud ascribed to processes of reality testing. He shows how we might find, in the metaphoric projections of our bodily interactions with our environments, a blending of the massive complex of our culture, language, and history that makes the world what it is to us.

Meaning making founded in metaphoric projections takes forms quite different from the rational thought conventionally accepted as the route to true meaning. Metaphors are analog rather than propositional forms of making meaning. They have a figurative, imaginative character unlike the rational, propositional thought central to the study of meaning in philosophy and linguistics. They are personal ways of making meaning rooted in our bodily activities, rather than impersonal thought modes that aim at meaning independent of our human embodiment. Johnson (1987) felicitously calls them structures of "embodied imagination."

Johnson does not speak to questions of self in the making of meaning in metaphoric projection, but his schemata of bodily activity meet our criteria for self. They are schemes of personally motivated action. In their metaphoric projections to other contexts, we experience a sense of spontaneity and aliveness. In his view, metaphor is a *personal* way of making meaning.

In this view, then, our structures of understanding are structures of selving. Body-based schemata are not impersonal drive structures, as in Freud's libidinal theory, but structures of personal action. They are not primitive thought modes as in Freud's conception of body-based, primary-process thought. Throughout our lives, our most basic ways of making sense occur in metaphoric projections of bodily I-activities.

Shapes of Meaning-Making Structures: Narratives

Ideas that narrative structures are the fundamental patterns by which we understand our worlds are converging from several directions. Sarbin (1986), disillusioned by the mechanistic frameworks that historically have guided social-psychological investigations, urges a program of research based on the notion that people impose narrative structures on the flow of experience. From the perspective of personality psychology, Bruner (1992) argues that the very forms of human cognitive organization are narrative patterns, not logical or categorical ones. From the standpoint of cognitive science, Schank and Abelson (1977) have proposed that our mental structures take the form of narrative scripts, mental schemes representing one's ways of performing certain activities, such as visiting the dentist or eating at a restaurant. In Stern's (1994) view from within his psychoanalytically informed infancy research, the earliest units of mental representation are "protonarrative envelopes." Within clinical psychoanalytic psychology, Schafer (1992) and Spence (1982), among others, vigorously champion the idea that we organize our experience in narrative terms and understand objects and events as they take their place in narratives.

In psychoanalytic psychology, influenced particularly by the views of Spence, questions of the narrative character of our understanding have taken a particular form. He argues that, if, as we must, we give up the objectivist view that objects and events are accurately registered in our minds and can be recovered in the course of analytic work, we must recognize that, although patients' memories and associations may be structured by events in the past, we cannot know those events. In our work with patients, we should ignore them. We should not attend to notions of historical truth but should instead develop a narrative truth, a life story constructed by patient and therapist. Its acceptability should be judged not on the basis of its accuracy in relation to actual events as in empirical sciences, but on its coherence and esthetic value as a narrative.

This view has been roundly criticized. Cohn (1992), speaking to the issue of congruence between a narrative account and the actualities to which it refers, argues cogently that there is no need to choose, as Spence (1982) does, between notions of absolute correspondence and no correspondence at all. For example, although histories, novels, journalistic reports, and clinical case histories are all narratives, they vary significantly in their intent to refer to actual events and the degree to which they are appropriately judged on that basis. Rorty (1993) and Bruner (1993) dispute Spence's notion that a focus on narrative limits evaluative criteria to narrative coherence and esthetics. They argue that widely varying forms of exploration are possible within narrative frameworks: empirical studies, anthropological investigations, the study of Freud's work, and examinations of clinical interaction.

Focusing directly on psychoanalysis itself, Wallace (1984) points out that the idea of historical truth as irrelevant to the exploration of people's lives is altogether contrary to the basic psychoanalytic proposition that the present is constituted by, and expresses, the past. Eagle (1984b) argues, more specifically, that in clinical work it is not enough to supply the patient with a new narrative of his or her life independent of actual events of that life. It is not congruent with clinical experience to propose, for example, that an early history of abuse and neglect or the death of one's family in the Holocaust is either unascertainable or irrelevant to the conduct of an analysis

It seems likely, now, that Spence's way of conceiving the place of narrative in psychoanalytic psychology will in the end be rejected. Must we then give up entirely the idea that narrative is the form in which we construct the meanings of events? Nelson's (1986) work in developmental psychology suggests that we need not. Like Lakoff and Johnson (1980), Nelson began very early in her work to raise questions about the long-standing theoretical commitments that have governed work in her field virtually from its beginnings. Research into cognitive development, like the study of meaning in linguistics and philosophy, has historically been based on the assumption that rational or propositional thought is fundamental to our understanding of reality. Investigators exploring developments in children's capacities for ascribing meaning to events focus on components of rational thought such as seriation, taxonomic categorization, making inferences, and deductive reasoning.

Nelson's informal observations suggested to her that there is a striking discrepancy between how well children deal with everyday experience and how poorly they do on such cognitive tasks. She began to think that cognitive research might be posing its questions in ways alien to children's actual modes of thinking. It seemed to her, increasingly, that children's understanding begins not with sensory registrations of experience elements that are subsequently organized by the rules of rational thought but in larger experience units.

Building on Schank and Abelson's (1977) conception of mental scripts, she began to explore the notion that children initially represent their experiences to themselves in schemata of whole-event sequences—(a birthday party, grocery shopping, having lunch at nursery school)—rather than experiencing elements that are subsequently organized into rational or experiential wholes. In long-term studies of children ranging in age from three to ten, short-term examinations of particular cognitive developments over a period of a few months (Nelson et al., 1986), and the exploration of development in a single child, Emily (Nelson, 1989) from about two to three-and-a-half years of age she and her colleagues study the structure of children's ways of making meaning of their experience and development and change in these structures.

In their ingenious research, they identify the basic structures of meaning making as event schemata[1] that take narrative form. From the earliest bedtime soliloquies of two-year-old Emily, through the productions of ten-year-olds, children structure their understanding of events in narrative sequences (when grandma came, lunch at nursery school, the birthday party). Nelson and her colleagues (1996) are able to show that such narrative schemes are established in the first instance of a novel event (a fire drill, going to the zoo), rather than being gradually built up from smaller units in successive episodes. In their extended explorations, the researchers show that event schemata are relevant to both memory of the past and planning for the future: they guide the encoding or retrieval of information from memory and provide a context for interpreting new experiences and forming plans for future activities. It is from their bodies of event schemata, the investigators show, that children begin to develop capacities for aspects of rational thought like seriation, categorization, and the making of inferences and predications.

That is, children first make meaning of their experiences in narrative terms. These narrative schemes have characteristics very similar to those of I-schemes. Like the I-schemes of nursing or grasping, they are action schemes. Nelson's conception, like that of Stern (1994), adds to the notion of I-schemes the explicit

---

[1] Nelson and I independently came to the term event as the basic unit of experience, and event schemes or schemata as their mental representations. Our interests have taken us in different directions, and it has been a pleasure for me to find that the implications of her work continue to be closely congruent with the those of my own.

recognition that these schemes represent the child's understanding of the *sequence* of activities that forms an episode of nursing, of going to the zoo, of a fire drill. Like I-schemes, Nelson's event schemata are schemes of personally motivated activity in which the child actively engages. In the sequence of Emily's monologues, the I-self quality of narrative schemes becomes particularly clear as Nelson traces the child's developing ability to report her memories, wishes, and perceptions in her soliloquies explicitly as I-activities.

Conceptualizing our basic ways of making meaning of our experience as narrative schemes by no means requires that we give up notions of congruence between schemes and the actualities to which they refer. The narrative schemes of Nelson's conception, like I-schemes, are products of the child's interaction with its world. They are structured by the developmental state of the child's cognitive system, on one hand, and the environmental phenomena with which the child is engaged, on the other. As in infants' establishment of nursing schemes, or those of grasping and visual tracking, children establish their notions of how the world works in interactions with it. The adequacy of their schemes of understanding is tested again and again in successive instantiations of the same scheme: if their expectations of, say, a nursing interaction, lunch at nursery school, or a trip to the zoo are not met, the scheme can be altered or elaborated to accommodate the new realities.

In such a view, I-schemes are narrative schemes. They are personally motivated schemes of interaction that take the form of narrative sequences. Thanks to the research of Nelson and her colleagues (1986, 1989), we can see beyond the paradigmatic action schemes we attribute to infancy to their more elaborated narrative expression in the bedtime soliloquies of a two- or three-year-old and the productions of children from ages three to ten.

In optimal development, we might surmise with Nelson, narrative schemes, elaborated and modulated in the course of self–world interactions, become increasingly adequate to our engagements with our environments. In less optimal circumstances, clinical experience leads us to believe, a person might, for reasons of anxiety, exclude some narrative configurations from the continuing interactions in which their modification can occur. These, then, form constellations that become the focus of clinical work aimed at their reintegration with the larger body of schemes that constitute our minds, and their modification to account more fully for our experiences of the world.

Dissociated Patterns of Meaning Making

Davies and Frawley (1994) illuminate meaning-making patterns in the traumatically dissociated experiences of adult survivors of childhood sexual abuse. They suggest that the dissociated experiences they observe do not occur as traumatic memories that must be abreacted, as might be expected in the context of drive theory, but occur instead as global relationship configurations. The structure and development of these relationship configurations closely match those of I-schemes.

Davies and Frawley suggest that these relational constellations are constructed in the abusive interactions of childhood. They are split off from the rest of the self and have not participated in the processes by which their various aspects are modulated, tested against reality, and integrated into the personality. They are expressed, often, as dramatic and frightening reenactments, in patients' day-to-day lives and in the transference––countertansference relationships of the therapeutic work. In successful clinical work, patients become able to articulate with increasing clarity the terrors, furies, misconceptions, and physical experiences embodied in these intrusive and initially baffling self–other interaction forms and to consider them in the contexts of their present lives, their histories, and their anticipations of the future.

Although Davies and Frawley do not explicitly speak of these reenactments as patients' ways of making meaning of their interactions, their clinical examples and discussions readily lend themselves to such a framework. In such terms, the reen-actments might be seen to reflect internal working models derived from abusive relationships that now pattern the patients' relationship expectations and behaviors. They are the metaphoric projections of traumatic-abuse situations that now govern their understanding of events in domains different from those in which the abuse occurred. They are narrative schemes by which the patients now understand their relationships to therapists and others.

The reenactments may also be seen as primitive I-scheme constellations, trauma-based relationship modes that pattern the patients'current ways of understanding their engagements with others, including their therapists. They seem to echo, with unusual clarity, aspects of early I-scheme structures.

Like primitive I-schemes, these isolated relationship constel-lations are activated as entire interactional configurations, each with its own emotional, cognitive, behavioral, and physiological components. A highly successful attorney, for example, unex-pectedly found that, whenever a demanding senior member of her firm asked to see her, she responded with terrified anticipa-tion. She suddenly felt herself to be physically little, like a five-year old. When she entered his office, her vaginal muscles began to contract. She felt pale, dizzy, shaky, and terrified of some unnamed danger. She was altogether unable to muster her characteristic assertiveness and spunk. As in the hypothesized I-scheme experiences of infancy, the patient seemed to under-stand her interactions with the senior partner in a scheme constellation that included the entire amalgam of her sense of herself (as little, a frightened five-year-old), her physical feelings (of pallor, shakiness, vaginal contraction), and her sense of the other (as dangerous in an unnameable way). It was a way of understanding interactions with a colleague that were strikingly disparate from her characteristically spunky and assertive way of behaving.

The self and nonself aspects of such dissociated I-scheme constellatons are incompletely integrated and differentiated. In a single clinical hour, for example, the meaning-making matrix can shift violently. At one moment, the patient appreciates the therapist as an idealized savior in relation to her needy, wounded, childhood self. A moment later, in a radical self–other reversal, she wildly abuses the therapist, now herself the furious and omnipotent adult haranguing the weary, guilt-ridden, and helpless therapist/child. Her part-selves as wounded child and as abusive adult are not integrated with one another; her sense of the therapist as ideal savior and as helpless child are quite separate. She does not securely differentiate herself as a child who has been abused by an adult, and within her reversing relationship units she perceives herself only as the complement to the other or the other as complement to herself.

Vestiges of the mind–body unity we attribute to early I-schemes appear to pervade these isolated relationship units. Body sensations easily intrude on relational activities. The meaning-making scheme the attorney activated in anticipation of meeting with the senior partner, for example, included vaginal contractions altogether inappropriate to the actual meeting she anticipated. Conversely, relational aspects of interaction structures also intrude on bodily experience. Often, in the observations of Davies and Frawley, bodily symptoms later understood as concomitants of early abuse relationships are taken by patients and physicians to represent actual bodily dysfunctions, with the result that the patients tend to have histories replete with undiagnosable illnesses, hospitalizations, and invasive but inconclusive medical procedures.

Patients' motivations in these undifferentiated, psychophysical ways of making meaning are intensely personal but carry little sense of I-ness. In the patient's wildly oscillating sense of herself as wounded child with savior therapist and ferocious adult with helpless therapist/child, her personal motivations are undeniable, but her activity appears as an enactment, with that term's implication of a limited sense of self. Similarly, the terror of the attorney on entering her superior's office is personally felt, but her experience seems to be of something alien having come over her, an intrusion from outside herself.

In the activation of even more primitive interaction templates, the experience mode itself appears to dominate, with virtually no articulation of its component parts. It appears to occur when the abuse has been particularly overwhelming (associated with early onset, high levels of sadism, and the centrality of the abuser in the child's life). In such cases the patient, sometimes within a single clinical hour, seems to be engulfed in unformulated experiential chaos. No articulation of self and therapist can be observed. The experience is of a timeless, objectless, selfless nightmare. When memories of such abuse return, they do not usually do so initially as memories of the self and the other involved in it, but, rather, in expressions of the relational mode itself, in radical and inexplicable mood shifts, panic attacks, or somatically experienced symptomatology.

Only gradually, in the transference engagements with the therapist, do the particulars of the abuse experience lend themselves to analytic exploration and integration with the larger body of self experience. In I-self terms, the patient simultaneously activates two disparate interaction modes toward the therapist: one, the dissociated I-scheme of the abusive relationship; the other, an ordinary, adult way of engaging the therapist in the present moment. As the patient is increasingly able to tolerate the conflicts between them, she can, like the hypothetical patient of the last chapter, more fully integrate her disparate part-selves and part-objects with one another, to ascribe aspects of interactions accurately to herself and the other, both as they occurred in the abusive relationships of her past and as she experiences them in her present life, and to achieve a more complete sense of her past and present engagements with her world as I-activities.

Summary

In this chapter, we have examined aspects of the constructivist notion that our I-selves pattern the ways we interpret our experience. We have explored confluences between the conception of I-schemes as our ways of making meaning and other conceptions originating within and outside psychoanalytic psychology.

We began with Freud's seminal proposal that people understand their experiences in patterns established in their earliest feeding and toileting activities and their ways of dealing with issues of sex difference and oedipal developments. We added other, more recent conceptions of ways to construe our meaning-making patterns. They include dynamic infant–mother interaction schemes, internal working models that organize our behavior in interpersonal relationships, metaphoric projections of schemes rooted in bodily activity, narrative forms established in the day-to-day activities of our lives and applied to our understanding of subsequent instances of those activities, and dissociated meaning-making patterns of abuse survivors.

The characteristics ascribed to meaning-making patterns in these perspectives arising in very different scholarly and clinical domains support the notion that I-schemes might be a useful way to construe such patterns. In almost all perspectives, meaning-making patterns are seen to represent personally motivated structures with varying degrees of I-experience: the *Ich*-activity of the Wolf Man's ferocious arguments, a man's insistence on speaking no matter what the occasion, the vestigial body pleasure of a successful balancing act in argument or money management, or Emily's growing mastery of the self referential "I" in her bedtime soliloquies. They are typically conceived, like I-schemes, as relational units, originating in infant feeding activities, in patterns of infant–mother attachment, in learning the body balance required by upright posture, in such everyday activities as having lunch at nursery school or going to the zoo.

Especially in abuse survivors' dissociated patterns of meaning making, we seem to see echoes of developmentally early I-schemes, interpretations of everyday events in global relationship units that represent entire complexes of cognition, affect, self and object aspects, action patterns, and physiological components. In some persons, no articulation of the various relationship components can at first be oberved, and no sense of I-ness. Others appear to show early stages of self integration and self–other differentiation in narrowly complementary relationships in which the self and other components are part-selves and part-objects whose meanings for the patient may shift radically from moment to moment, and, where integration and differentiation are a little more fully established, a sense that they are I-activities.

Constructivist notions of our ways of making meaning run counter to traditional objectivist ones. In psychoanalytic psychology, they invite a move away from Freud's conception that meanings made of events in terms of oral, anal, or sex differences are distorted meanings imposed on accurate, perception-based registrations of events. They suggest, instead, that we cannot count on discovering veridical, sense-based meanings in any areas of our lives. All meaning is constructed, whether of such relatively conflict-free events as having lunch at nursery school or of anxiety-laden experiences of sexual abuse.

To propose that all meaning is constructed, however, does not at all imply that any meaning is as good as any other. Rather, like the infant who modifies its nursing scheme to secure the nipple more adequately or children in nursery school who adaptively modify their schemes of having lunch in successive instances of these activities, we ordinarily construct and reconstruct our I-schemes to take into account more fully the actual events of our lives. In the isolated I-scheme constellations of abuse survivors we can observe the consequences of failure in this typical adaptation process.

In chapter 4 we begin to explore I-self activity that carries little subjective experience of I-ness. In Eagle's (1984) and Loewald's (1980) terms, it is experience attributed to the id. In Ogden's, it is central to the paranoid-schizoid experience mode. In I-self terms, it is experience rooted in discrete, undifferentiated I-scheme constellations.

4 SELVING WITHOUT A SENSE OF I-NESS——I

ENCODING EXPERIENCE IN GLOBAL I-SCHEMES

Chapter 3 closed with patterns of meaning making that seem to echo aspects of developmentally early I-schemes. Like primitive self schemes,[1] the dissociated ways of encoding experience that Davies and Frawley (1994) found in adult survivors of childhood sexual abuse appear to be isolated interaction modes, unintegrated with the patients' usual ways of going about things. They are patterns that represent entire complexes of cognition, affect, self and object aspects, action patterns, and physiological components.

At the extreme, the self aspects of these interaction patterns may be almost entirely unarticulated. Patients may experience overwhelming mood states with no sense of I-ness at all. With somewhat greater differentiation, self aspects appear as part-

---

[1] Fully discrete I-schemes can exist only briefly in the course of their initial establishment. They virtually always occur as I-scheme constellations. Therefore, to avoid repetition, the term I-scheme, unless otherwise specified, implies a constellation of schemes.

selves tightly bound to complementary part-objects. These part-selves seem to be markedly unstable, the patient often veering wildly from the enactment of one concatenation of thoughts-feelings-attitudes-actions to the expression of a radically different one.

Only gradually, as patients activate these dissociated patterns of selving in transference–countertransference engagements with their therapists, do they articulate their various aspects and integrate them with the larger bodies of their experience. It is in these integration processes that their feelings, thoughts, and actions increasingly carry a sense of I-ness.

Our ways of encoding events in which a subjective sense of self is missing or is, at best, rudimentary is the focus of this chapter and the next. As is suggested by abuse patients' dissociated interaction patterns, self–world engagements lacking a sense of I-ness are patterned quite differently from those that carry a full sense of first-person engagement. In psychoanalytic psychology, experience lacking a subjective sense of I-ness reflects the first of two periods into which early development is traditionally divided. In Freud's terms, the earlier period is that of the id (*das Es*) from which the ego (*das Ich*) subsequently emerges. In object relational terms, it is the period prior to the establishment of a whole self in relation to whole objects.

We can place the dividing point at about two years of age. Although Freud does not identify the id-ego transition in terms of the child's age, the phenomena he attributes to the period of transition are known to be achieved at around that time. He associates it with the beginning of language use (Freud, 1925); now, as the child begins to seek libidinal objects, the oedipal period begins. Objects with bound cathexes, the permanent objects of other literatures, replace experience in which the meanings of objects change with every dynamic shift (Freud, 1911). Experimental action in the mind can now precede motor action (Freud, 1911). The child begins to establish "a reservation for imaginative activities" (the realm of pretend and symbolic play) that lead later to poetic and artistic creation (Freud, 1925). And, finally, as suggested by Freud's terms *das Es* and *das Ich*, it is the time when the child becomes able to ascribe its perceptions, feelings, and activities to an experiencing self as "I," "me," or "mine."

Object relations frameworks draw attention to the establishment of a whole self differentiated from whole-objects by about this time. In Mahler, Pine, and Bergman's (1975) work it is the period of rapprochement, the final stage of the early childhood establishment of an independent self. Other empirical work (Lewis and Brooks-Gunn, 1979) shows that children's growing sense of "me" and "mine" culminates at about this time in their ability to use the self referential "I," and Piagetian research (Flavell, 1963) has demonstrated the establishment of permanent objects by about 18 to 24 months.

In these two chapters, we explore clinically observed ways of selving in later life that appear to echo the first of these mental organizations. In Freud's conception, they have the characteristics of the id or the unconscious; object relational perspectives attend to their part-self, part-other natures. Ogden explores them as aspects of the paranoid-schizoid experience mode. Freud's clinical observations led him to conceive of the id as an organization in which thoughts, feelings, and actions carry no subjective sense of I-ness. Impulses are enacted rather than remembered. Contrary wishes exist side by side without connection or contradiction. Thought is governed by the primary processes. Thought and what is thought about are not distinguished. The experience itself is the criterion for reality.

Object relational perspectives invite attention to self organization rooted in this early period as an array of part-selves incompletely differentiated from part-objects. They suggest that the self and object aspects of primitive self–other bonds are unstable, easily reversing their interaction positions in oscillations of introjection and projection. Little attention has been paid, in these frameworks, to people's subjective sense of I-ness. In what follows, I suggest that it is limited to the extent that self and objects are part-selves and part-objects.

In Ogden's (1986) work the paranoid-schizoid experience mode echoes this early period. Ogden himself does not ascribe the paranoid-schizoid and depressive modes to sucessive developmental periods, as Klein did.[2] However, his identification of the paranoid-schizoid mode with ways of understanding one's experience that lack a sense of I-ness, and his attributing to that mode other phenomena that Freud ascribed to the id and object relations theorists ascribed to the period of part-selves and part-objects, suggest that his delineations of paranoid-schizoid ways of interpreting one's experience can usefully be seen as another vantage point from which experience rooted in the earliest developmental period might be explored.

The I-self concept puts forward still another perspective. It suggests that we have a subjective sense of I-ness in our self–world engagements (perceiving, thinking, feeling, acting) to the extent that we differentiate the self and nonself aspects of our I-schemes and integrate them across schemes into an increasingly complex whole self in relation to whole objects.

Selving with at most a rudimentary sense of I-ness occurs when the articulation of self and other is absent or minimal. Then, as in the nursing schemes of infancy whose self and non-self components remain inchoate, people understand events in terms of global interaction patterns. They might, like the abuse patients of Davies and Frawley (1994), experience those events only as overwhelming mood states. In less horrific circumstances, people might be plagued by an ego-alien urge or compulsion or, in everyday life, experience themselves as "just going with the flow" or immersed in "the usual goings on," with little or no sense of their own part in the activity.[3]

---

[2] In psychoanalytic psychology, we have not resolved the question of whether these experience modes are properly identified with severe disturbance or are among everyone's ways of going at things. The dissociated experiences of abuse survivors might suggest the former; Ogden's views support the latter. For the present, the matter is left undecided here. In the material that follows we will find some examples taken from severe disturbance and others from the experience of children and adults without clinical involvement.

[3] Winnicott (1963) may have been describing a very pleasurable form of this experience mode in his notion of a state of "going on being." As Ogden (1991) points out, it speaks to a feeling of aliveness without reference to either subject or object.

This chapter and the next explore dimensions of this way of conceiving self experience lacking a sense of I-ness. The first attends predominantly to its object relational context. It explores, in various contexts, how experience without a sense of I-ness might usefully be seen as experience in global schemes whose self and nonself aspects are not articulated, rather than experience in merged part-self–part-object representational units.

The second proposes ways in which it might accommodate the phenomena Freud included in his conception of the id. The conceptual contrast in chapter 5 is between viewing "id" phenomena as drive dominated and uninfluenced by the external world, on one hand, and, on the other, seeing them as people's ways of encoding experience in I-scheme constellations that are (relatively) unintegrated with the larger body of their I-selves.

A Limited Sense of I-ness and of the Nonself World

The Sense of I-ness and Id Impulses

Loewald (1980) uses the example of the woman plagued by a compulsion to murder her child to illustrate the development in analysis from experience with no sense of I-ness to that which is experienced as personally motivated. The compulsion feels to the woman like a frightening, impersonal urge that intrudes on her ordinary sense of herself. In the course of analysis, she begins to understand that she harbors feelings of hate against the child. These feelings are related to a disturbed relation with her husband and, in turn, to certain feelings toward her father. In the course of analysis, as she integrates them into a "linkage of personal motivations," what she had experienced as an impersonal, compelling force becomes a part of her introspectable self.

In traditional drive theory, these clinical observations might be understood as a complex of id impulses erupting from the unconscious and being gradually integrated into the ego. In Loewald's relational terms, as in those of the I-self conception, the woman's feelings toward her child, her husband, and her father are patterned, from the beginning, in personally motivated relationship configurations, but they do not initially carry a subjective sense of I-ness. It is in the integration of her feelings with the larger body of her experience that they increasingly attain first-person character.

I-Experience and the Paranoid-Schizoid Mode

Ogden (1986) radically enlarges the experiential field in which we might observe the lack of a sense of I-ness in people's self experience. It does not occur only as an id intrusion in the otherwise undisturbed *Ich* of Freud's ego: it is central to an entire pattern of experiencing.

The paranoid-schizoid mode, in Ogden's view, carries only a rudimentary first-person quality. One has little feeling of personal aliveness: things seem simply to occur, rather than being accomplished personally. There is little or no sense, however subtle, that one is thinking one's thoughts and feeling one's feelings rather than living in a state of reflexive reactivity. One does not have a sense of oneself as the author of desire or interpreter of events.

The paranoid-schizoid way of selving is not reflective. One has no sense of having a personal point of view or perspective. It is as though a man were to say "It's hot" without the unspoken sense that "I am aware that it feels hot to me." A woman might experience "He's dangerous" rather than "I am aware that I feel him to be dangerous." The absence of self reflection might be expressed in the omission of personal pronouns in a person's speech, as when a man reports the day's activities as "went to school today . . . no luck . . . teacher's a prick . . . hate him" (p. 49).

Ogden highlights the link between a subjective sense of I-ness and the differentiation of symbol from that which is symbolized. First-person experience, he suggests, ordinarily fills the space between thought and what is thought about. It is this space in which one thinks one's thoughts, lives in one's body, dreams one's dreams, and places one's experience in contexts of past and future. In the paranoid-schizoid mode, that space is absent. Instead, people experience events as happenings in which they are immersed.

Without the distinction between symbol and symbolized, feelings or thoughts come upon one as forces by which one feels suffocated, penetrated, attacked, or unprotected. They might occur as a "wave" of depression, or an irresistible "need" to binge, to take drugs, or to put oneself in physical danger. One might, like Loewald's (1980) patient, feel "plagued" by an urge to kill one's child.

A person can be observed to interpret his experience in terms of particular codes or templates, but in this experience mode he himself has little sense of doing so. Like the parents of Fonagy et al.'s (1993) studies, who might unreflectively enact their established internal working models with their children, patients in the paranoid-schizoid mode have no sense of themselves as casting their experience in a particular light. The event is what it is: there is no vantage point from which to observe it from more than one perspective or to consider it in the light of previous experience.

Experience is discontinuous in the paranoid-schizoid mode. Different facets of experience do not stand in relation to one another. Instead, like Kernberg's (1966) patient, who *was* (subjectively) a longing child with an all-loving grown-up at one moment and a depreciated little boy with a harsh adult at another, the individual is a prisoner of each immediate state of mind, though he does not experience it as only a state of mind. When differences occur, they are dealt with through magic transformation rather than compromise. Ambivalence cannot occur, because one feeling is altogether withdrawn when a new emotional state is entered; the one replaces the other rather than being integrated with it.

The goal of psychoanalysis is, in Ogden's view as in Loewald's, the transformation of that which has been experienced as an impersonal occurrence into experience that has a quality of I-ness.

Self (and Nonself) Experience in Undifferentiated, Discrete I-Schemes

The I-self concept adds the notion that self and other emerge together from global I-schemes. Therefore, a person's lack of a sense of I-ness in an activity must be accompanied by an equally limited sense of its nonself aspects. When the patients Davies and Frawley (1994) describe encoded their abuse experiences only in terms of dissociated mood states, they had neither a sense of I-ness nor an articulated sense of the abusive other. We expect that Kernberg's (1966) patient, who had little sense that he was interpreting his experiences with Kernberg in two sharply different ways, had an equally limited sense that Kernberg viewed their interactions in one light or another. To the extent that people are "just going with the flow," say, in a meeting or a party, with little sense of their own agentic participation, they can be expected to have an equally incomplete sense of other participants' activities as agentic.

In this view, the lack of a sense of I-ness that Ogden (1986) attributes to the paranoid-schizoid mode must be accompanied by an equally incomplete sense of the nonself world. When, for example, people have no sense of personal aliveness, they will have no sense of a lively world with which they are engaged. When it seems to them that "things simply occur," rather than being accomplished personally, it will seem to them, too, that others are involved in such 'occurrences' rather than being actively engaged in personal accomplishment. With little sense that they are thinking their thoughts and feeling their feelings, they are likely to have little sense of others as thinking, feeling persons.

This view can also add new dimensions to our understanding of the compulsion Loewald describes. In his conception, his patient's compulsion to kill her child is a constellation of relationship forms isolated from the larger body of her psychic organization. In I-self terms, it is, like the mood states of the abuse survivors, self experience in which the self and nonself aspects of relatively discrete relationship forms (I-schemes) are inchoate.

Loewald (1980) emphasizes that the woman feels her compulsion as an impersonal urge with no quality of I-ness. The I-self view invites us to notice, too, that she has no articulated sense of the nonself aspects of the relevant relationship configurations (the parts she ascribes to her husband and father). The intense, personally motivated interaction mode (the compulsive urge) predominates; both its self and its nonself components remain implicit.

As she becomes aware of and integrates her feelings toward her husband and father into a "linkage of personal motivations," the woman more completely senses the I-ness of her feelings toward them. We expect that she also articulates the nonself aspects of these I-schemes (her sense of the contributions of her husband and father to her interactions with them) to exactly the same degree.

Now, too, the dominance of the isolated I-scheme is ended. The woman is no longer overwhelmed by a compulsive urge that seems to come from outside her. The I-schemes that constituted the compulsion, now integrated with the large body of her I-self networks, come under her aegis. Rather than feeling herself to be subject to an ego-alien compulsion, she has a sense of herself at the center of her life, actively remembering, feeling, thinking, and acting in her engagements with others, to whom she attributes their own independent subjectivity.

The Rudimentary Articulation of Self (and Nonself) Within Global Schemes

The notion that experience without differentiation of self and nonself occurs in discrete, global schemes, rather than in the fused, self–other units commonly postulated in object relations perspectives, invites a new look at the primitive self–other bonds that have long been a focus of exploration in the latter frameworks.

Some examples:

In the wildly fluctuating transference–countertransference interactions Davies and Frawley (1994) describe, in which a rudimentary differentiation of self and nonself can be observed, a patient might at one moment be helpless-child-with-savior-therapist, and at the next, in a self–other reversal within this interaction mode, be furious-adult-with-helpless-child-therapist.

In a clinical hour with me, a young woman (Ms. F) makes of me a "nothing" whose words have no effect on her. She imperiously turns me into a pattern of light and shade with figure and ground reversed, as in a photographic negative. In a few moments, she whitens: she herself now feels unreal, disconnected, helpless. Now I have the power and, as she feels it, have made "nothing" of her.

A young boy (Gary), in tears of fury, threatens me with his fist and shouts, "OK, Mr. Knuckles! . . . ," although I am a woman and he is the one with the threatening knuckles.

Observations such as these are typically described, in object relational terms, as reflecting relational units in which a part-self and a part-object are merged with one another. In such fused self–other units, characteristics are attributed to self and other in oscillating processes of introjection and projection.

If, instead, we take the global I-scheme as primary, we focus on the relational mode (abusive, destructively dismissive, threatening) rather than on the self and object representations. We would expect that, if we could observe no self–other differentiation at all in the patients' understandings of these incidents, we would find not even more thoroughly fused self and object representations, but rather, experiences of undifferentiated mood states or urges, perhaps a frightening sense of impending abuse, a destructive urge, or an inexplicable sense of threat, with no identification of self or other.

In fact, these patients do distinguish self and nonself components of the interactions (abusing and abused, dismissive and dismissed, threatening and threatened). Their sense of I-ness, and of the other, however, is strikingly unstable. In an easy reversal of the parts they ascribe to self and to other, an abused patient may at one moment be abused-child-of-therapist/abuser and, at the next, furious-abuser-of-therapist/child; Ms. F becomes dismissive-destroyer-of-unwanted-therapist and almost immediately feels herself to be destroyed-unwanted-patient-of-dismissive-therapist; Gary engages me at one moment as furious-threatener-of-hapless-therapist, but then senses himself as threatened-victim-of-Mr.-Knuckles/therapist.

It seems, in the I-self perspective, that these ways of selving, in which people distinguish the self and nonself aspects of their activities in rudimentary ways, move well beyond self experience in which they make no such distinctions and have no sense of I-ness at all. Self and other, however, remain embedded in discrete I-scheme constellations: they are only abusing and abused, dismissing and dismissed, threatening and threatened, within the narrow bounds of a single mode of interaction. The person's sense of I-ness fluctuates erratically from one pole of the interaction to the other. A stable sense of oneself, with a network of I-schemes flexibly available for interpreting one's experience and acting in one's world, is not yet established, or is, at the moment, not in use.[4]

Attribution and Misattribution of Agency and Affect in Undifferentiated self Experience

Attempts to understand people's misattributions of feelings and motives to themselves and others have been central to psycho-

---

[4] Representations of self and other coordinate to these dynamic self aspects are not centrally in focus here. We can see, however, that in these incidents they are correspondingly incomplete and unstable. Ms. F can, for a moment at

analysis from its beginnings.[5] In traditional drive theory, they are explored as drive derivatives structured in processes of conflict and defense. Object relational explorations have focused particularly on the attribution of affect and motive within primitive self–other bonds and in their alternating attribution to self and other in projection and introjection processes

The notion that self and other might be only minimally articulated aspects of discrete perceptual-cognitive-affective agentic schemes raises new possibilities for observation. It suggests that, in some circumstances, people might attribute feelings and motives that we see from the outside as their own, not only to themselves or others, but to broader aspects of their experience. Like some abuse survivors, they may sense their feelings and motives only as overwhelming mood states that pervade an entire event. With minimal articulation of self (and other), people might encode them as coming from outside, in the waves of anxiety or needs to binge that Ogden describes or in the compulsion of Loewald's example, or as somehow coming from inside, perhaps as immanent powers of magical creativity. With somewhat greater articulation of self and other, they might, like Ms. F or Gary, erratically ascribe their feelings to themselves or another within a particular interaction mode.

Two studies exploring affect development (Fitzpatrick, 1985) and affect maturity (Thompson, 1986) lend support to this idea. Fitzpatrick attempted to show a developmental line, in three- to six-year-olds, from children's ascription of their feelings to

---

least, defend herself against my words by making me a transparency; and, when, in the dynamic self–other reversal, she interprets our interaction as one in which she is being utterly dismissed, her imperious sense of herself easily succumbs to terrifying feelings of unreality and disconnectedness. In his uncertain sense of his own and my gendered reality, Gary can attribute maleness to me, and in his minimal sense of our separateness he can call me Mr. Knuckles although *he* is threatening *me* with his fist.

[5] The discussion here does not attend to the dynamic processes that might result in particular attributions of feelings and motives to oneself or another. It speaks only to the underlying structures postulated in the drive, object relations, and I-self perspectives within which such attributions might occur.

entire global events, to a recognition of them as their own subjective states. She asked the children to describe affect events ("a
time when you were happy," "a time when you were afraid")
and inquired about the location of the "happy" and "afraid"
feelings.

The children easily identified affect events (happy: "when
I'm riding my tricycle," "when it was Christmas"; afraid: "if a
lion was in my room at night," "if there was a monster"). The
older children typically located their "happy" or "afraid" feelings in themselves as subjective states. Younger children, in con-
strast, might attribute feelings to the "happy" or "afraid" event
as a whole. The happy feeling, for example, might be located in
Christmas, with its entire amalgam of opening presents, hug-
ging grandparents, seeing Christmas tree lights, playing with
cousins.

Interestingly, Fitzpatrick also found what seemed to her to
reflect a transitional period. In this mode, children (mis)-
ascribed feelings to various event components rather than to the
event as a whole but did not yet securely attribute them to
themselves. The happy feeling, a child might say, is "in my tricycle" or "in my mouth;" the scared feeling is "in the monster,"
or "in the lion's mouth."

In this transitional mode, Fitzpatrick shows, the residual
importance of the discrete, global event remains central. Even as
they began to ascribe "happy" and "afraid" feelings to various
event components, the children seemed to retain the belief that
fundamentally feelings belong globally to the particular activity as a whole. The happy feeling was not an affective disposition of the tricycle to be manifested on various occasions, but
was there only "when I'm riding my tricycle." Fear was not in
the mouth of the lion when he was walking around in the jun-
gle, but only in the lion-in-my-room-at-night event.

Only when children ascribed feelings securely to themselves
as subjective states did affects lose their event-specific character
and become personal affective dispositions that might be activated or not, in various situations. The I-self conception would

predict, beyond the work of this study, that, coordinately, children would at this point also ascribe feelings to others as subjective states whose expression was specific to them and under their own control.

Thompson (1986) explored levels of affect maturity in the TAT stories of moderately disturbed adults evaluated in an outpatient clinic. Storytellers at higher levels of affect maturity, like the older children of Fitzpatrick's study, attributed emotions to personal subjective states. Affect at the lowest of her five levels of affect maturity, by contrast, seemed to echo clinically observed global I-scheme experience and the global affect ascription of Fitzpatrick's (1985) younger children.

A storyteller might say, in response to a TAT card, "There looks to be a pensive mood [in the pictured event]" or "That's a sad picture," without further ascription of the sadness to one or other of the story characters. In such stories, Thompson observes, affect had an atmospheric or moodlike quality. It was as though the character were immersed in an affect-event, perhaps like the happiness-suffused Christmas of Fitzpatrick's younger children, the "happenings" Ogden (1986) describes, or, at the extreme, the nightmarish mood states of abuse survivors.

When, at this level, storytellers did attribute feelings differentially to the pictured characters, they seemed, like Fitzpatrick's (1985) transitional group, to do so uncertainly and within the single global event. The storyteller who ascribed a "pensive mood" to the pictured event as a whole, for example, went on to say that the it might "be filled with some anxiety, could involve the interrelationship between them [the two persons pictured in TAT 6BM] or a third party . . . it's hard for him to confront, or they're confronting a third issue together. Or maybe it's hard for her to tell him, or vice versa" (Thompson, 1986, p. 219).

Such vacillation might readily be seen, in object-relational terms, as evidence of alternating introjection–projection processes in a fused part-self–part-other unit. That perspective, however, does not easily accommodate the storyteller's original attribution of the "pensive mood" to the picture as a whole. It seems, rather, that for this storyteller, the pensive mood, the anxiety, or the difficulty of confronting an issue defined the event as a whole; the attribution of these feeling states to one or another individual, or to two individuals in concert, was secondary and as unstable as, in the stress of the moment, it was for Gary or Ms. F, or, in her transference–countertransference exchanges, for the abuse patient.

Self (and Other) Embedded in Global Schemes

Two observations illustrate, with particular vividness, ways in which global schemes may take priority over one's sense of oneself and of the other in the interpretation of events. An incident in the clinical work with Gary (whose "OK, Mr. Knuckles!" illustrated his easy reversal of self and nonself within his furiously threatening interaction with me) provides one example. A form of storytelling that occurs in our (Fast et al., 1996) empirical studies of self organization offers another.

For Gary, in residential treatment, his parents' weekly visit was of vital importance. If for some reason (bad roads, illness at home) a visit could not occur exactly as planned, he became frantic. He was terrified that his parents had deserted him. He expressed his fears poignantly in images of death, starvation, and being lost. It seemed clear to us that he desperately needed and wanted his parents. When, on one occasion. they would not be coming, he was predictably panic stricken. Quite suddenly, though, elation replaced panic: he had solved the problem! He made what was to us an astonishing proposal. If the Emersons, who lived in his home town, in his very own neighborhood, were to come at the appointed time and visit with him in the room in which he and his parents usually spent their time together, he could have his parents' visit. It was not that a visit with the Emersons might be an alternative to his regular parents' visit. Not at all. At least in the terror of the moment, it seemed to him that if the Emersons came from his own neighborhood, from his own city, at the regular time, and they visited in the proper place, his Parents' Visit could take place.

His desperate need for his parents invited an object relational perspective in which his separation from his parents was central. In his, at least momentary, view, however, the "problem" could be solved without his parents. It was the *event* that was required, the Parents' Visit event, not the parents themselves.

In this way of encoding their experience, people's sense of self and of the other, or of a self–other unit, seems to be entirely secondary to their sense of the global event. Comfort occurs when the "happening"—the Parents' Visit or other familiar event—unfolds in its ordinary way; it seems to matter less who the interaction participants are.

This global way of interpreting events seems also to be reflected in our empirical explorations of self organization. In a series of studies (Fast et al., 1996) we asked people, given TAT-like instructions, to tell a story about a pair of pictures of a woman in two different situations. In one she is with an older woman; in the other she is with a young child. At higher levels of self organization, the storytellers might perceive the woman as a working mother, in various ways dealing with the conflicting demands of a job (first picture) and motherhood (second picture). In their stories, the interaction participants (the young woman, the older woman, the child) were primary. The narratives focused on the characters' differing ways of behaving on the basis of their own personalities, their relations to the others, and their complementary or conflicting wishes and goals in the pictured events. At the lowest level, on the other hand, the interaction mode seemed to dominate. A storyteller might say, for example, "Here [Woman with Older Woman] she is *with* her mother. Here she *is* the mother [Woman with Child]. It's the same . . . loving and trusting in both [not further explained]."

Like Gary's belief that he could have his Parents' Visit if he could enact the familiar interaction sequence, even if it was his neighbors rather than his parents who visited, this story form initially baffled us. Gradually, however, we became convinced that the sameness of the two events resided in the interaction mode (in this case, loving and trusting). It was not that the young woman loved and trusted her mother in her own personal ways and that, in ways appropriate to a quite different relationship, she loved and trusted her child. Rather, for this storyteller, the two pictured events were the same: a global "loving and trusting" defined them both. That an adult woman's ways of loving her own mother and her ways of loving her young child could not be the same was no more relevant for this storyteller than that his parents and the Emersons were different people was, in the moment, for Gary.

Global I-Schemes Define the (Part) Self and the (Part) Other

In chapter 2, we proposed, in tune with Piaget and Winnicott, that when I-schemes are relatively unintegrated, scheme components (e.g., the bottle, the rocker, the mother of the nursing event) do not have stable meanings but are defined and redefined by the schemes in which they occur. In Winnicott's (1971) paradigmatic example, the self of the positive infant–mother interaction is the good self in the infant's experience; the self of the negative interaction is the bad self. Initially, the good self and the bad self are not the same self for the infant.

This conception has two parts. The first has been extensively explored in object relations paradigms: the self of primitive relationships is an array of unintegrated part-selves. The second, not easily accommodated in the conception of the self as rooted in a fused self–other unit, has received little attention: in primitive relationships the discrete interaction modes (affectively positive and negative in Winnicott's example) define and redefine the self (as good and bad) in differing events.

The first, self organization in terms of discrete part-selves, has been elaborated with particular vividness in Deutsch's (1942) "as-if" personalities, Greenson's (1958) "screen identities," and, as discussed earlier, Kernberg's (1966) borderline personality organization.

Deutsch, for example, describes one patient, an artist, who adopted totally and very quickly the style and mode of perception of her teacher; but, when she became the student of another teacher, her adoption of his very different approach was equally total and rapid. No trace of her previous orientation remained in her work with the second teacher; the two artistic identities remained altogether discrete. It seemed to Deutsch that in this patient, as in other as-if personality organizations she had observed, each identity was elaborated in an intense "adhesive" relationship, and, when one relationship was broken off, a new one, just as tightly complementary, replaced it.

Greenson (1938) observes that persons with "screen identities" seem to have multiple identities as though they were different selves with different people. Even with one person they might display different identities in the context of contrary feelings of love and hate. For such a person, like Winnicott's infant, the person loved is not the same person as the one hated. Instead, feelings of love and hate alternate, and when the person loves he or she retains no dim memory of any previous hatred.

Kernberg's (1966) borderline patientseems, similarly, to have had discrete identities, among them, the rejected, depreciated little boy in relation to a harsh and haughty adult and another as a longing, guilt-ridden child with an all-forgiving, all-loving grown-up. Like Greenson's patients, Kernberg's could not integrate his positively and negatively toned experiences; when he felt negatively toward Kernberg he could hardly recall his earlier positive views, and when he idealized Kernberg he could hardly recall his earlier negative feelings.

The second aspect of Winnicott's (1971) example, the notion that these part-selves are defined by the interaction in which they occur, is more easily accommodated in the idea of global interaction modes than in the concept of fused self–other units as the base from which the self develops. It is temptingly implied in Deutsch's (1942) observation that her patient's disparate artist identities were elaborated in separate, tightly complementary relationships; in Greenson's (1958) comment that people with screen identities are different selves with different people; and in Kernberg's (1966) sense that in his patient's two interaction modes he was expressing two distinct selves or ego states unconnected with one another.

The way the relationship mode might define and redefine self and other can be seen more explicitly in a small, but particularly vivid, clinical vignette; a characteristic of stories told at low self integration levels; and another incident in Gary's attempts at coping with his world.

First, the vignette. In an informal discussion, an analyst described what to her had been a startling experience. Recently she had moved her office from one location to another some blocks away. In her first meeting with a patient (Mr. A) in the new office, she was puzzled by what seemed his odd behavior. In Mr. A's analysis the details of his family relationships had been the focus of extended work. Now, however, as he spoke of family members, he identified them by name and elaborated familiar events as though he were describing them for the first time. It was as though his entire going-to-see-my-analyst I-scheme constellaton had changed now that he had to go to a different place, enter by a different door and elevator, and meet his analyst in a different room. Although objectively he was meeting with the same analyst as before, it was as though, in his experience of the moment, he could not know with clarity that he and his analyst in the new office (or in the new going-to-see-my-analyst scheme) were the same persons as in the old. In ways of which he was hardly aware, his sense seemed to be of a new analysis, one in which previously shared knowledges would have to be newly established, the old relationship newly made.

Second, in our empirical explorations of self integration (Fast et al., 1996), too, it seems that when storytellers at the lowest integration levels interpret one situation as different from another, they may, in the second situation, view the protagonist as now a different self. We presented storytellers with pictures of the same person in two very different events (in one pairing, the same man is shown in one picture as poor and dejected, in another as well-to-do, smartly groomed, and confident; in another pairing, the woman with older woman and woman with child pictures, in both of which the woman is well-groomed, were followed by a picture in which the same woman is alone, disheveled, her clothes in disarray, a drink in her hand).

At higher levels of self integration, storytellers tend to integrate the pictured events in both series historically. The man, for example, might be seen to be poor but musically talented. He achieves popular and financial success but is haunted all his life by his early poverty. The woman, now a working mother, frequented sleazy bars in her rebellious college years. Now, older and wiser, she struggles to raise a child by herself, hampered financially by not having completed her education.

At the lowest levels of self organization, however, storytellers might imply that, in the newly pictured event, the character has become a new person rather than being the same person in different circumstances. They might say of the male figure, that, having orginally been a poor man and having become wealthy, "he goes on as this guy" as though he were not the same "guy" as before. The woman, perhaps a devoted mother in their first story and now in a bar, "has lost herself" or "can't find herself."

Curiously, Mr. A's experience seems almost the obverse of Gary's in ways that match two apparently contrary story forms at the lowest self integration levels. For Gary, if the Emersons came from the *same* street, from the same town, and they visited in the same place at the right time, his Parents' Visit could occur, even with people who were not his parents. For Mr. A, if he went by a *different* route and to a different office to see the same analyst, he could not be sure that he and the analyst still shared the history of their previous work together.

At the lowest self integration levels, similarly, we see two opposed ways of integrating the pictured events. On one hand, if the pictured events are not very disparate (e.g., woman with an older woman and then with a child), storytellers tend to find them the same although the interaction participants are different (e.g., loving and trusting in both). On the other hand, if the pictured events are sharply disparate (the man poor and rich, the woman well-functioning and dissolute), storytellers may find them different: the protagonist is a new self in the new event.

The underlying factor that unites these apparently contrary ways of encoding clinical and storytelling events seems to be the dominance of the isolated, global I-scheme constellaton. In one circumstance (the Parents' Visit; 'loving and trusting in both'), the patient and the storyteller define the event as the same and ignore the differences among the participants. In the other (the new office; the poor man, rich man; and the woman well groomed and dissolute pictures), they define the two events as different and ignore the fact that the interaction participants are the same.

For a third illustration, another incident in Gary's experience, again involving the treasured Parents' Visit, seems to reflect an intrapsychic conflict between two disparate I-schemes activated simultaneously, each defining the self in a radically different way. It was a situation that might have caused another child easily resolvable ambivalence—Gary found the problems insurmountable.

It began with the possibility of an unexpected visit home. Gary was overjoyed. Suddenly, however, his mood changed. He became panic stricken and glassy eyed; familiar images of a starving child and a lost dog took the place of his pleasurable anticipations. He had realized that his parents were to pick him up at the very time of his regular Parents' Visit. On one hand, therefore, he would be going home with his parents; on the other, he would be missing his Parents' Visit.

Exhilaration alternated with despair. He could not integrate his scheme-specific sense of himself as loved-boy-going-home with his identity as abandoned-boy-without-a-Parents'-Visit.

The sense of himself sitting snugly in the car, riding home with his parents, could not modify his sense of himself as a lost boy with no parents in the context of the missed Parents' Visit. His part-object parents of the coming-to-take-him-home event could not modulate his panic sense of the abandoning parents of the no-Parents'-Visit event.

For a few moments at a time he could juxtapose the two events and be pleased about going home. Almost immediately, however, this comforting integration faltered: again he could only feel himself alternately to be the loved-boy of the going-home event, and the abandoned-boy of the missed Parents' Visit scheme. His parents, reciprocally, seemed to him only the loving-parents of going-home and the lost-parents of the missing Parents'-Visit event.

Horrid Empty Spaces

Finally, the notion that experience without a sense of I-ness occurs when people understand events in terms of discrete, global schemes suggests a way to understand the "annihilation fears" often found in people whose self experience is significantly unintegrated and undifferentiated.

Ogden (1986) speaks of such fear as a sense that one's entire existence is somehow negated, not a fear of actual death, but a feeling as if one were to disappear without a trace in unbounded space. A patient of Loewald's (1977) described it as a sense of himself as lifeless, without feelings or thoughts, and of the therapist as a strange unattached figure. In Balint's (1955) evocative phrase, one's world seems a "horrid empty space" to which one has no connection, rather than a "friendly expanse" inviting engagement. To a highly competent young woman in my clinical practice (Ms. G), successful in a demanding occupation, it seemed as though in such experiences she entered an emptiness, unable to find a sense of reality in any anticipated activity. She felt herself constantly on a tightrope, anxiously organizing her day, fearful of being precipitated into that self less, boundaryless void. Gary, trying repeatedly to make me understand how it felt, described it variously as a "ghost feeling," "like not being attached to anything," "like a machine with all the wires loose," "like a machine not working but you're still alive."

The incident Loewald (1977) describes occurred when his patient saw him with his arm in a sling after a slight accident. It was then that he was overcome by a sense of his own deadness and an utter detachment from a now alien Loewald.

Ms. G tended to be plagued by such fears if an expected phone call did not occur exactly on time or if she knocked on an apartment mate's door and, unexpectedly, no one answered. When a meeting ended early, she could not use this free time in her busy schedule as a (small) friendly expanse in which to relax; instead her feeling was of a horrid empty space, herself unbalanced, shaking inside, and without connection to a familiar world.

Gary's "ghost" feelings permeated his days. They might occur when he waited at the elevator for his parents to arrive. When, as must often happen, the elevator door opened but his parents did not emerge, he saw . . . nothingness! When he and I were to meet in an office other than our usual one, his ghost terror was such that he found it difficult even to walk steadily. After intense anxiety, which he could specify only as being about his brother's becoming a teenager on his approaching 13th birthday, he was able to clarify his feelings with a question: "How would my brother know [when he became a teenager] what he liked for breakfast?" It was as though his brother, in this new identity, would be in so unfamiliar a world that he would have no way of dealing with even such ordinary affairs as choosing his breakfast cereal.

Thus far, clinical explorations provide us with no more than beginning understandings of the content and structure of such fears. Object relations perspectives encourage the view that annihilation fears reflect the loss of an object to which one is symbiotically attached. That view, however, does not easily account for the occurrence of annihilation fears when no object loss can be identified, when, for example, one's analyst is present though wearing a sling, or one unexpectedly has free time, or one is meeting with one's therapist in a different office. Nor does it in any obvious way account for the annihilation experience as patients describe it: their sense of being lifeless or as insubstantial as a ghost or of being unconnected to a world that they see as a horrid empty space; or, more globally, a sense that their entire existence is negated, or that they are no more than a machine with all its wires loose, "not working but you're still alive."

The I-self conception invites speculation in another direction, rooted in the notion that I-schemes are both our selves in relation to our nonself worlds and our ways of making meaning of our experience. In the ordinary course of development, people integrate their I-schemes into a network of templates or codes flexibly available to them in their personal understandings of their self–world engagements. Unexpected events, if not too extreme, might throw a person off balance a little but would not require much more than a minor shift in interpretation.

When self integration is significantly limited, however, experience is likely to be disjunctive. When unexpected situations occur (unscheduled free time, the analyst wearing a sling, parents not emerging from the elevator) people might have no network of alternate interpretations smoothly and flexibly available to them. Instead, they might be, for the moment at least, altogether without codes or templates with which to interpret what is happening and, in that absence, without a sense of themselves or of the world.

Might it be the horrific sense of having no self and no way at all of making sense of things that Gary was trying to express in his metaphor of "a machine not working but you're still alive"? Perhaps Ogden's patient was trying to describe something like this in the notion of a person's entire existence being negated or of disappearing without a trace in unbounded space. Maybe it was a sense of being utterly baffled at the sight of his analyst with a sling and being suddenly devoid of any sense of either himself or of the world that Loewald's patient was trying to convey when he spoke of his experience of deadness, of having no thoughts or feelings, and of Loewald as alien.

Summary

This is the first of two chapters that explore aspects of selving in which the sense of I-ness is absent or rudimentary. Psychoanalytic conceptions and empirical investigations alike suggest that experience without a sense of I-ness is rooted developmentally in the first 18 to 24 months of life. Psychoanalytically, this is the period of the id, of part-selves and part-objects, and, perhaps, of the paranoid-schizoid position.

The I-self concept suggests that people have a sense of I-ness in their activities (perceiving, thinking, feeling, doing) to the extent that they have differentiated and integrated the self aspects of initially global, discrete I-schemes. When the self aspects of schemes are only minimally articulated, people interpret their experience in terms of global schemes (mood states, urges, or feelings of "going with the flow") with little or no sense of their personal contribution to these experiences.

Here we focus predominantly on this view of experience without a sense of I-ness in its object relational context. The basic relational unit, in this view, is not a merged part-self–part-other representation, but a dynamic I-scheme whose self and nonself aspects are at most minimally articulated. This view invites the notion that, because self and other emerge together from global schemes, every lack of a sense of I-ness in one's activities is matched by an equally limited sense of the lively reality of others. (An abuse survivor with no sense of I-ness in her dissociated mood states will also have no sense of the abusive other; when one is "going with the flow" one has little sense of others as more actively engaged.)

To the extent that people have not integrated and differentiated the self and nonself aspects of their interaction schemes, they interpret their self–world engagements in terms of global I-schemes. The primitive self–other bonds, explored in major object relations perspectives as representations of a fused self and other, vulnerable to oscillations of introjection and projection, are seen in this view as rudimentary and unstable articulations of self and other within discrete I-schemes. Affect and agency, initially undifferentiated aspects of global I-schemes, are not ascribed only to the part-self or part-other of a self–other unit, but may be experienced as permeating entire events, as coming from outside oneself, or being somehow immanent in one's experience or, in unstable ways, as an aspect of oneself or another.

In people's activities, global I-schemes, their ways of going about things, are central. It might matter more that an event like a Parents' Visit go off as scheduled than that one is interacting with one's actual parents. Conversely, if circumstances change (a meeting with a therapist occurs in a different office; a poor man becomes rich), one might not retain a secure sense that the persons involved have not also changed their identities.

In the context of discrete, global I-scheme experience, people may be vulnerable to "annihilation fears" when confronted with an unexpected event. Without a complexly integrated network of I-schemes to account for the unexpected, they may have no code or template at all to account for the "new" event. Their experience, then, might be one of utter bafflement that includes the loss of all sense of their own reality and relation to a nonself world.

5 SELVING WITHOUT A SENSE OF I-NESS—II

ID EXPERIENCE IN GLOBAL I-SCHEMES

This chapter continues the attempt to show how the idea that we encode our experience in terms of unintegrated I-schemes might accommodate psychoanalytic ways of thinking about self experience without a sense of I-ness, now in the context of classical psychoanalytic theory.

Experience without a sense of I-ness lay at the heart of Freud's "depth" psychology. His explorations of the ego-alien or disavowed experience that he observed in emotional disorders led him to the view that the id (non-*Ich*) ways of selving which dominate the unconscious are patterned quite differently from ego (*Ich*) ways. His observations convinced him that, when people experience events without a sense of I-ness, affects rather than rational thought govern their understanding and their actions. Contrary ideas exist together without connection or contradiction. Objects are without stable meanings and may stand for one another if their dynamic meanings for the individual are the same. Thought is structured in terms of the primary rather than the secondary processes. Experience is timeless, without placement in one's personal history or in anticipations of the future. People enact their impulses rather than acting mentally without accompanying motor action. Thoughts are taken for reality.

In his conception of the id (*das Es*), the theoretical frame for his observations, non-I experience is body (drive) based, without contact with the external world. In the first generation of psychoanalysis, explorations of these "depths" of experience found in the unconscious were central to psychoanalytic psychology. Today, however, the clinical observations Freud organized in his conception of the id and the unconscious can easily be neglected. The growth of ego psychology in this country turned attention from the depth psychology in which psychoanalysis began to the complex processes by which people integrate their wishes and fears with the demands of the external world. Moreover, widely accepted critiques of Freud's *conceptions* of the id and the unconscious in the context of ego-psychological explorations, (Apfelbaum, 1966; Gill, 1967; Klein, 1976; Eagle, 1984a) seem also to have encouraged an ignoring of the *observations* on which Freud built his conception.

With the more recent burgeoning of relational perspectives, interest has again turned in new directions. In those contexts, phenomena of the "id" and the "unconscious," still identified with the drives and drive derivatives, are not easily accommodated. They increasingly seem to belong to an outdated one-person psychology and to be of no more than historical interest.

Here Davies (1996) has made an important contribution by proposing a way of thinking about the unconscious from a relational perspective. This "relational unconscious" is composed of multiple, incompatible self states, each of which is a relational unit. The notion of irreconcilable self states invites a dissociation-based rather than a repression-based conception of the unconscious. Davies argues convincingly that this was Freud's early way of understanding unconscious experience and that he only later replaced it by a repression-based one.

The two views suggest very different relations between consciousness and unconsciousness. Davies's view emphasizes vertical splits in the ego; those splits permit the dynamic interplay of multiply organized centers of awareness and agency, in which conscious and unconscious refer to the nonintegration of incompatible relational schemata. Freud's later view is a hierarchical model of horizontal splits between the conscious, the preconscious, and the unconscious. Davies urges that a return to Freud's early dissociation perspective provides a useful framework to accommodate the growing body of clinical observation of adult sequelae of early trauma and, more generally, offers a model for exploring and understanding unconscious experience in relational terms.

Davies's model is conguent in major ways with the concept of the I-self. The units she proposes are centers of self experience. They are relational units. The central factor in the relation of the unconscious and conscious is not the degree to which a wish or impulse takes into account the external world; rather, it is the isolation of relational self schemata or their integration with the larger networks of people's minds.

To meet Freud's criteria for unconscious (id) experience, now, we must begin to show that our ways of going about things in unintegrated self schemata or I-schemes are patterned by elements Freud ascribes to the id. Can we observe activity modes that Freud might describe in id terms when Gary threatens me with his fist and, in a moment, calls me Mr. Knuckles? When storytellers see a change of identity with a change of circumstance, can we expect that their thought patterns might reflect id characteristics? Are the dissociated mood states of the abuse survivors Davies and Frawley (1994) describe id formations in Freud's sense?

Experience Is Affect Dominated

Freud's objectivist view equates the external world with objective reality and rational thought. It is the world of ego activity, the world of experience that carries a sense of I-ness. Affects, in contrast, reflect the essence of id activity. They are body-based drive derivatives, intense, all-engulfing, voracious. They are fundamentally unrelated to the external world of reality. Only as they come under the control of the rational *Ich*, is their expression modified to conform to the external world. Only then do feelings carry a sense of I-ness.

In this view, the nightmare panics of abuse survivors are id experiences unrelated to the external world. The woman's compulsive urge to kill her child, in Loewald's example, is an ego-alien eruption from the primordial id. Gary's terror at missing his Parents' Visit can be understood as a product of unconscious drives, uncontrolled by the ego of objective reality. When Ms. F dismissively turns me into a negative, nothing but a pattern of light and shade, her destructive fury is an expression of bodily drive derivatives unmodulated by contact with the external world.

In the I-self form of Davies's (1996) dissociation-based unconscious, in contrast, there is no time in our lives when our feelings are entirely endogenous, taking no account of the "external" world. From the beginning of life, they are patterned in our self–world engagements. Our ways of taking in a movie "orally" may be rooted in our early nursing interactions; a person's constant fear of being abandoned, perhaps in relationships with a depressed mother; a woman's urge to kill her child, as in Loewald's example, in early conflicts with her father; a woman's nightmare terror, in early abusive interactions.

The dissociation model also takes a different view of ego-alien affect in people's later lives. It does not view it as an eruption from the "depths" as in the hierarchical repression model. Rather, from a dissociation perspective, disavowed ways of feeling, like those fully accepted as aspects of oneself, occur in current self–world engagements. A woman's urge to kill her child occurs in her present interactions with her child, side by side with her other, more benign ways of interacting with it. Ms. F's transforming me into an insubstantial negative was a ferocious

engagement with me in the present, concurrent with, but subjectively isolated from, her other contemporary ways of interacting
with me.

In this view, clinical or developmental progress occurs not by
bringing primitive, drive-based affects under the control of the
ego but, rather, by the integration of isolated ways of going
about things with the larger network of the individual's I-
scheme constellations. If Gary could have integrated his aban-
doned-boy-with-no-Parents'-Visit scheme with his loved-boy-
going-home one, the feeling patterns of both schemes might
have been altered by modulation with one another. It is when,
in Loewald's example, the woman brings to the foreground, and
integrates, the various aspects of her difficult relations with her
father and her husband that her urge to kill her child dissipates.
As Ms. F could integrate her destructive wishes with the larger
body of her feelings toward me, she found, partly to her dismay,
that her capacity to nullify me had deserted her; it had been
modified out of recognition by integration into more complex
constellations of feelings.

Contrary Experiences Exist Together Without Connection or Contradiction

In the conventional, repression-based view of the unconscious,
impulses and wishes coexist, without connection or contradiction, in a drive-derivative, endogenous world unconnected to
the external one. The form taken by these impulses and wishes
in the unconscious has not achieved generally agreed on definition. As they come under the aegis of the reality-oriented ego,
they are seen to be organized in processes loosely attributed to
the "integrative or synthetic function of the ego."

In his seminal discussion of borderline disorders, Kernberg
(1966) introduces an alternative way to understand unconnected

ego-alien experiences. He proposes that in severe character disorders and borderline conditions we observe a kind of split in
the ego. Like the patient who alternately experienced himself as
a longing, guilt-ridden child with an all-forgiving, all-loving
grown-up, and as a rejected, depreciated little boy in relation to
a harsh and haughty adult, these patients tend to experience
contradictory ego states or relationship units quite divorced
from one another. Each is temporarily ego syntonic; but, when
the other experience form comes to the fore, these patients feel
emotionally divorced from the previous one. It is no longer part
of their psychic reality.

Kernberg emphasizes that, in his view, these defensive organizations are different from repressive ones. The two contradictory experience forms are both self–world engagements; neither
occurs without connection to external reality. Both are conscious
and ego syntonic at one moment and subjectively without psychic reality at another. He proposes that they are primitive
defenses typical of severe disorders, distinct from the repressive
ones found in neuroses.

Kernberg's view of defensive splitting is congruent in major
ways with Davies's (1996) conception of a dissociative relational
unconscious. The units of experience are relationship units dissociated from one another: when the patient experiences himself
as longing child with loving grown-up, his incompatible experience of himself as depreciated child with haughty adult has little reality for him. In Davies's terms, the split between them is
vertical, not horizontal. Both modes of selving are self–world
engagements; neither is divorced from external reality. The
terms conscious and unconscious do not refer to hierarchically
ordered domains of experience. They speak to the individual's
subjective sense of one relationship constellation as ego syntonic
(carrying a sense of I-ness) at one moment, and as ego alien
(with no sense of psychic reality or of I-ness) at another, the
same being true of the contrary relationship mode.

However, in Davies's view, as in the I-self concept, the notion
of dissociation is a replacement for, rather than an addition to,

that of repression. The distinction to be drawn is not between two modes of defense or two relations between conscious and unconscious. It is a contrast of two theoretical perspectives aimed at making sense of the same body of clinical observation.

In this view, then, the incompatible "impulses" or "wishes" that exist side by side without connection or perceived contradiction are relational units or I-scheme constellations. They might include a young girl's relations to her mother as alternately deadly competitors and the best of friends; the hypothetical patient's contrasting interactions with his colleague as awe struck admirer of the clever business man and righteously superior critic of his evident inability keep his tie straight and his shoes tied; or an abuse survivor's incompatible feelings of herself as helpless-child-with-loved-therapist and as furious-abuser-with-helpless-child-therapist.

Each of these is a self–world engagement in no way divorced from the external world. Each is a way of selving, though perhaps carrying no more than a rudimentary sense of I-ness. Neither is a denizen of a hierarchically "deep" unconscious; each may be ego syntonic at one time and subjectively without psychic reality at another. Clinical progress does not involve integrating one or another of such interaction modes with a higher order, reality-related ego; it involves integrating the initially incompatible I-scheme constellations with one another and with the larger body of the individual's dynamic self.

Objects Are Without Stable Meanings

Freud observed clinically that the same object might have different meanings for a person in different circumstances, or, conversely, that two different objects might stand for one another if their dynamic meanings for the individual are the same. The grieving man of my example might see himself at different moments as utterly desolate, a playboy suddenly free, or a zombie dead to all he has loved. For Greenson's (1958) patient, the same friend was subjectively a different person when the patient loved him and when he hated him. In their stories to pictures of a man or woman in very different circumstances, storytellers might suggest that the initially poor man, now rich, "goes on as this guy," as though he were now a different "guy," or that the well-groomed woman, now dissolute, had "lost her identity," or couldn't "find herself," as though she were not the same self any more.

Conversely, if the dynamic meaning is the same, quite different objects might have the same meaning for the individual. For the Wolf Man of Freud's (1918) major case study, his mother's and sister's money, the relationships among God, Jesus, Joseph, and Mary, and a worrisome blemish on his nose, all had meanings concerned with his anxieties about who could and who could not give birth. A man for whom "everything that is not me is dirt" might understand such varied matters as the smell of his own feces and the silverware at his place setting in a restaurant, in the same terms, as either dirt or not.

Freud framed observations such as these in terms of drive cathexes of object representations. In his objectivist perspective, objects are accurately registered in the mind. Any instability in their meanings results from the distorting influence of the bodily drives. Therefore, when the same object (a friend, oneself, a pictured man or woman) has different meanings for an individual in different circumstances, these shifts in meaning are ascribed to the mobile cathexes of unconscious drives. Likewise, when a number of different objects have the same meaning for a person, this distortion of their perception-based meaning results from the drive domination of the person's perception or thought. In this way, the dynamic (drive derivative) wish to be able to give birth distorts the Wolf Man's (Freud, 1918) views of his mother's and sister's money, the Holy Family, and a spot on his nose. The anal-drive-based "everything that is not me is dirt" might, as noted, structure a man's experience of the smell of his feces, his fork and knife in a restaurant.

The meanings of objects recover their stability with the removal of dynamic interferences, at which point the individual regains their objectively accurate meanings—now feces are mere bodily wastes; a fork is just a fork; a friend is the same person whatever one's momentary feelings toward him; the meanings of God, Joseph, Mary, and Jesus lose their drive-based distortions.

In the I-self view, too, the same object might have different meanings, and different objects might stand for one another if their dynamic meaning is the same. This instability of meaning, however, is not a consequence of dynamic forces divorced from the external world acting on accurate, perception-based representations; it is the consequence of the nonintegration of initially discrete I-schemes. In the beginning, in this constructivist view, object representations (like self representations) are fully defined by the dynamic schemes in which they occur (as the mother, the rocker, the baby's own sucking are defined by their place in the nursing activity). These, however, are not bodily schemes that have an exclusively distorting influence on representations. They are dynamic schemes structured by the infant's active and adaptive self–world engagements. The initially inchoate self and object representations are patterned by these adaptive activities.

These representations are unstable to the degree that the initially discrete schemes are not integrated. They are defined and redefined by the dynamic schemes in which they occur (the mothers of the comfortable and uncomfortable holding situations are subjectively not the same mothers for the infants). Similarly, different objects might have the same meaning if their place in a dynamic scheme is the same (a nipple, a wooden block, and a blanket edge may stand for one another in the infant's sucking activities).

In later life, too, the meanings of objects are "unstable" to the extent that the I-schemes that define them are not integrated with one another. Gary's contrary images of his parents as loving and as abandoning are a function of their place in his disparate and unintegrated schemes of No-Parents'-Visit, on one hand, and My-Parents-Taking-Me-Home, on the other. Mr. A's need to tell his therapist again about his family relationships when he meets with her in a new office is not a function of drive distortions of his relationship to her, but of his definition of her as familiar with them in his earlier going-to-see-my-analyst scheme and his redefinition of her as unfamiliar with them in the context of the new and not yet integrated one.

Throughout life, object representations (like representations of self) are defined by complex arrays of dynamic schemes. Maturity or sophistication in one's representations is defined not by the degree to which representations are free of dynamic influence but, on the contrary, by the number and refinement of the dynamic schemes that define them. It is the increase in the number of dynamic schemes and the complexity of their integration that enlarge the subtlety and complexity with which we are able to understand our worlds.

The Primary-Process Mode Prevails

In Freud's view, as in the conceptions of Western thought generally, rational thought (the secondary process) is the standard for intellectual maturity. It reflects the rational organization of the real world.

As Freud observed clinically, however, non-I (id) experience is not organized in rational patterns but occurs as experience in an immediate situation. Dream images provide one example. The situation-like events underlying symptoms provide others (a woman reimagines herself at her dying father's bedside; the Wolf Man reevokes watching the mating of sheep on a Russian

farm). Such thought forms advance in analogue rather than logical progressions; movement is from one experienced event to
another that is affectively analogous to it. In such a thought
sequence, for example, the hypothetical patient of chapter 2
associates, in a series of idealization–contempt patterns, to his
current observations about the cleverness but careless grooming
of his colleague, then to memories of an envied, ladykiller friend
who, however, had not made good, and, further, to thoughts
about the therapist's insightful remark, on one hand, and her
failure as a grower of plants, on the other.

In Freud's conception, these situation-like thought modes
characterize the non-I experience of the id or unconscious.
Unlike secondary-process thought, they do not reflect the rational organization of external reality; they are expressions of the
bodily drives. They are primary processes, appropriately primitive in early development and pathologically so in later life. In
development, they are typical of children's thought before they
turn to the external world at about age two and establish the
reality-related secondary processes. In later disturbance, those
ideas or impulses that are not brought into contact with the
external world retain their primary-process, situationlike structure in the unconscious of later life.

Recent constructivist perspectives raise questions about
event-centered thought as primitive and as unrelated to the
external world. The metaphoric projections that Johnson (1987)
proposes as the ways we typically structure our thought and
action are situation-like patterns established in such early
self–world engagements as achieving upright balance. The children of Nelson's (1986) studies organized their experience cognitively in developmentally appropriate event schemes.
Bowlby's Internal Working models are interaction patterns that
structure people's parent–child relationships for good or ill.
Congruently, the I-self conception proposes that I-schemes patterned by our self–world engagements are ways we make
meaning of our worlds.

Even Freud himself at times conceived of mature thought as

thought that is both experience patterned (and in that sense belongs to the primary processes) and also fully adapted to the external world. He proposed, as a significant development from id to ego, the individual's capacity for "trial actions" in the mind before putting them into action. But trial actions concern adaptive self–world engagements, although they do not occur in rational (secondary-process) modes of thought. They differ from primitive, analogue thought, not in taking a rational or logical form but in differentiating the mental and motor aspects of an idea expressed in analogue terms.

It seems, then, that we must not take event-patterned or analogue thought forms as a criterion for unconcious or id experience. Though they may, as Freud observed. take primitive forms in early development or later disturbance, they may also be adaptive and occur at the highest levels of maturity.

Experience Is Timeless

Freud (1900) observed that in neuroses, and especially in hysteria, experiences in the unconscious have no connection to time: they are not ordered temporally and are not altered by the passage of time. "A humiliation that was experienced thirty years ago acts exacly like a fresh one throughout the thirty years. . . . As soon as the memory of it is touched, it springs into life again" (p. 578).

In Freud's repression-based model, such memories are held in the unconscious. They press upward toward awareness and are countered by repressive defenses. It is here that psychotherapy intervenes. It is in the laborious work of bringing such a memory to consciousness, to *Ich*-experience modes, that it can be dealt with finally and then be forgotten.

In tune with a dissociation-based view of the unconscious, Ogden (1986) observes this timelessness, not in experiences that emerge from the depths of psychic structure, but as it may occur pervasively in people's day-to-day self–world engagements. He suggests, evocatively, that in the paranoid-schizoid mode one lives in a series of discrete presents. A new experience with someone is not integrated with the old. Instead, the old is discarded without being dealt with "finally," and the new experience replaces it as the "real" truth only now recognized. One has no sense of one's own or others' historical selves, oneself as being more or less the same person over time in relation to other people, who also continue to be the same people. In clinical work, no stable shared experience of the history of the patient–analyst relationship provides a framework for the present experience.

Gary, contending still again with a parental absence, vividly illustrates this ahistorical encoding of events when I-scheme constellations remain discrete, not integrated into the larger body of *Ich* experiencing. On one occasion his parents were away on an extended vacation. Anticipating his distress, they attempted to help him place their absence in a manageable time frame. They talked extensively with him about where they would be and about their coming home. They sent daily postcards to remind him of their continuing love. His caregivers also spoke reassuringly of his parents' activities and of their approaching return. Nevertheless, Gary was inconsolable. He "knew" that his parents had been shot. He would never see them again.

In our work, as in his living situation, we spoke of his parents' activities, their concern for him, and their return. He could only intermittently engage my suggestion that we try to remember later how frightened he was now, although his parents were in fact alive and well: then, perhaps, he need not be so afraid another time.

His parents returned. Gary burst into my office, exulting, "They're not shot anymore!" A new "present" had replaced the old. His "anymore" alluded to a juxtaposition of past and present, but he was utterly unable to integrate them, to reinterpret his earlier belief in the light of present knowledge (to know that he was wrong about them having been shot). His experience remained ahistorical. He could only know that his parents had been dead and were not dead anymore. His unrealistic belief was not dealt with in any final way. Like the humiliating experience of Freud's (1900) example, it could, and did, recur again and again when circumstances evoked his separation fears.

Finally, the dissociation-based notion that timelessness in one's experience is related to the vertical split among I-schemes is given some support by our studies of self integration (Fast et al., 1996). At higher levels of self integration, time continua are typically central to people's stories. In response to the male picture pair (the man poor and dejected in one picture, well-to-do and smartly groomed in the other), for example, storytellers might describe the man as poor but musically talented and achieving success in the course of various achievements and setbacks. They might identify him as a lonely immigrant who works hard, becomes well-to-do, and brings his family to join him. They might see him as moving from poverty to wealth, but haunted throughout his life by his early penury.

At low self integration levels that precluded their maintaining a continuity of the protagonist's identity from circumstance to circumstance, on the other hand, storytellers also tended to interpret pictured events with a striking absence of time frames. They might not indicate any time continuum at all. A storyteller might say, "Here [first picture] he is an immigrant . . . sad and alone. Here [second picture] he is at a fancy party going over to chat with someone."

No time relation is specified between the two story aspects. In Ogden's terms they are two "presents" without continuity. The story teller is not oriented to showing the place of the man's sadness and loneliness in relation to his participation in the party. His "going over to chat with someone" does not impel the storyteller to explain the connection between the protagonist being "sad and alone" and attending "a fancy party." The experience, as told, is timeless, without the historical framework in which, in 'Ich' ways, we organize our lives.

In this dissociation-based view of the unconscious, then, timelessness is a function of vertical splits in experience, the isolation of I-scheme constellations, rather than the horizontal split of Freud's repression model. In such split-off experiences, an old humiliation might be reexperienced as a present self–world engagement, temporarily engulfing one's sense of oneself, but existing side by side with other, quite different I-scheme constellations. In Ogden's example, when a new experience with someone replaces an old one as the newly recognized "truth," the old view, rather than being integrated with it, now subjectively without psychic reality, is not relegated to unconscious depths. It coexists with the new "truth," subject to being evoked again, and once more "newly" recognized "truth" when circumstances change. Gary's "knowledge" that his parents are shot loses reality for him in the context of his parents' return and is in that sense unconscious. That idea, however, not integrated with his other I-schemes and disposed of in a final way as unrealistic, is subject to being reevoked unchanged on subsequent occasions.

Impulses Are Acted Out Rather Than Remembered, and Thoughts Are Taken for Reality

These two characteristics of experience without a sense of I-ness suggest a further way in which the notion of unintegrated I-schemes might accommodate the phenomena Freud ascribed to the id and the unconscious. That is, the nonintegration of I-schemes also results in nondifferentiation within them. Specifically, in the I-self view, acting out one's impulses and taking one's thoughts for reality reflect failures in the differentiation of the mental and physical aspects of global, unintegrated I-schemes.

Freud (1914) introduced his discussion of remembering and acting out with the observation that "the patient does not say that he remembers that he used to be defiant and critical towards his parents' authority; instead, he behaves in that way to the doctor" (p. 150). In clinical work, Freud observed, the more intense the affect (the drive influences), the more one can expect acting out rather than remembering.

Loewald (1976), in a discussion largely congruent with the I-self conception, suggests, in disagreement with Freud, that acting out and remembering are both forms of memory, one enactive, the other representational. Representational memory develops in processes by which interactions within the original mother–child matrix are transmuted into internal interactions that constitute the individual psyche. In later life, people enact that which they exclude from the overall context of meaning.

The I-self version of Davies's (1996) dissociation-based unconscious suggests that enactive rather than representational memory is likely to occur to the extent that I-scheme constellations are not integrated with larger, networks of selving, and as a result the mental and physical aspects of experience are not differentiated. From the beginning, in the I-self conception, experience occurs in sensorimotor schemes: the mental and physical aspects of our self–world engagements are not differentiated. "Memory" occurs in the reevocation of an established scheme (e.g., of nursing) in a new circumstance (a subsequent instance of nursing is patterned by the "memory" of the former one).

It is through the integration of I-schemes that the mental and physical aspects of such schemes become differentiated, and it is with that differentiation that we become increasingly able to act mentally with or without acting physically. In development, this capacity makes possible the "trial action" that signals the transition from id to ego. In later life, to the extent that I-scheme constellations are isolated, excluded from the overall context of meaning, enactment rather than remembering free of physical action is likely to occur. Then, like Freud's (1914) patient, a person might not "remember" how he acted toward his parents but instead will behave that way toward the therapist in the clinical hour.

The same nondifferentiation of the mental and physical accounts, in the I-self conception, for taking one's thoughts for reality. In Freud's view, on the other hand, it is an aspect of the repression-based unconscious. Drive-based wishes determine one's interpretations of events; external reality is left out of account. One's (drive-based) experiencing of an event is, subjectively, the sole criterion for its reality.

In ways congruent with a dissociation-based notion of the unconscious, Ogden (1986) shows that "taking one's thoughts for reality" occurs in people's active engagements with their worlds. He accounts for it, as does the I-self conception, as a failure to differentiate the symbol from the symbolized (the mental from the physical). In such experience, he observes, events speak for themselves; one has no sense of interpreting them. Perception is unmediated by a sense of oneself as the creator of meanings. Instead experience carries instant and absolute conviction; there is no room to entertain ideas, to play with alternative perspectives or interpretations. The experience itself is the criterion for reality.

People do not stop taking their experience uncritically for reality by becoming engaged with the external world. In the experience forms Ogden describes, they *are* involved with their worlds. That achievement depends on their differentiating the symbol from the symbolized, thought from the actualities being thought about. In I-self terms this differentiation occurs with the integration of the isolated I-schemes with the larger networks of their ways of selving.

Summary

This chapter is the second of two chapters that explore aspects of selving without a sense of I-ness. It suggests ways in which we might conceive the phenomena Freud attributed to the id as ways of selving in unintegrated I-schemes. In this discussion,

Davies's (1996) conception of a relational unconscious is central. It is a dissociation-based rather than a repression-based framework, a conception of vertical splits among incompatible relational schemata rather than of horizontal splits in a hierarchically organized structure of conscious, preconscious, and unconscious experience.

This concept is strongly congruent with the I-self notion that experiencing without a sense of I-ness (id experience) occurs in isolated I-schemes, ones that are not integrated with the larger networks of individuals' ways of selving. This chapter has shown how the I-scheme version of Davies's relational unconscious might begin to accommodate the observations Freud framed in his notions of the id and the unconscious. It focuses on some of the characteristics Freud found to be central in primitive experience modes: affects dominate experience; contrary ideas exist without connection or contradiction; objects are without stable meanings; thought is dominated by the primary processes; experience is timeless; impulses are acted out rather than remembered; and thoughts are taken for reality.

It suggests that unconscious (id) experiences are not endogenous, patterned by the bodily drives, but are patterned in individuals' engagements with their worlds. They do not occur in people's lives as eruptions from the depths of psychic structure, but are self–world engagements that are split off from the individual's other ways of selving. People's ways of going about things in their everyday activities exist side by side with their other self–world engagements but are subjectively isolated and carry little or no sense of I-ness. These actions occur in the primary-process mode; they are eventlike organizations of experience in which thought advances in analogue rather than logical progressions from one situation to another that is emotionally analogous to it. In partial disagreement with Freud, however, recent explorations of cognitive structure (Internal Working Models, metaphoric projection, event schemata) suggest that this analogue thought mode can be found not only in primitive thought modes but throughout the range of cognitive functioning to the highest levels of sophistication.

In thought without a sense of I-ness (*das Es*), objects are without stable meaning, not because perceptually given accurate representations of reality have been distorted by drive cathexes, but because they are defined and redefined by the isolated I-scheme constellations in which they occur. Development and clinical progress are not accomplished by freeing an accurate, reality-based representation from distorting dynamic forces, but as scheme integrations place it in an increasingly large and stable nexus of dynamic I-schemes. Experience is timeless, not because it is an isolated wish or impulse forcing its way upward from the unconscious, but because, in their self–world engagements, people do not integrate their disparate experience modes; they live in a series of isolated presents in which one experience replaces another rather than being integrated with it.

In id experience, people act out their impulses rather than remembering them, but not, as Freud would have it, because acting out takes the place of remembering. In the I-self view, acting out and remembering are both forms of memory. In the first, the mental and physical aspects of global schemes are not differentiated; in the second, mental–physical differentiation permits people to act mentally with or without concurrent physical action. Similarly, in id experience people take their thoughts for reality, not because the thoughts are drive based and do not take external reality into account, but because people have not differentiated thought and what is being thought about. Then, as Ogden (1986) details, events speak for themselves; people have no sense that they are interpreting them. A thought or perception carries instant and absolute conviction. In Freud's terms, the experience itself is the criterion for reality.

6 FROM SELVING WITHOUT A SENSE OF I-NESS TO FIRST-PERSON EXPERIENCING—I

TOWARD AN INTERNAL WORLD

In this chapter and the next we turn from experience forms in which we have little or no sense of I-ness to those in which first-person experience is firmly established. The capacity for I-experience identifies the second of the two periods into which psychoanalytic psychology divides early development. In Freud's terms, *das Ich* (the ego) now takes center stage. In major object relations perspectives whole-object relationships replace interactions of part-selves with part-objects. From Ogden's perspective, the depressive experience mode of adulthood echoes the developments of this period.

As we turn to first-person ways of perceiving, thinking, feeling, and acting, we might imagine that, in development, the capacity for the self referential "I" simply emerges at around age two; in clinical work, one must merely attach a sense of I-ness to experience that has been disavowed. But if we can rely on Freud's and Ogden's observations and those made in object relations contexts, people's first-person experience is organized in markedly different ways from that in which they have little or no sense of themselves as agents in their thinking and doing.

One aspect of this new organization is central to various perspectives within psychoanalytic psychology: I-experience occurs when people have a sense of living in an internal world of self experience coordinate to a nonself external world. Freud's clinical observations led him to suggest that *Ich* experiencing occurs when people have internal worlds in which "trial action" is possible, and he associated the establishment of the *Ich* with the child's capacity for taking into account the external world in its thoughts and actions. Ogden more explicitly emphasizes the intimate relations between people's sense of I-ness and their establishment of an inner space of thought distinct from what is thought about. In object relations perspectives, the notion of a whole-self and whole-objects is not explicitly equated with people's internal and external worlds, but that equation seems typically to be accepted informally.

The notion that selving with a sense of I-ness is associated with having an inner world distinct from the outer world carries an intuitive validity, but the concepts of inner and outer remain slippery. Two disparate meanings are typically conflated. On one hand, the internal and external worlds are identified with self and nonself; on the other, the internal world of I-experience is the arena of thought, feeling, and imagination that is distinct from the individual's bodily sensations and actions and from actual objects and events. It is the intrapsychic world of trial action and of thought distinct from the objects of thought.

These two meanings are not at all congruent. Self distinct from nonself speaks to questions of accurately attributing thoughts, feelings, and actions to oneself and to others (and the nonhuman world). The differentiated self is by no means isomorphic with the inner world of mental activity. Our intrapsychic worlds are established not by the differentiation of self and other, but as realms of mental I-experience distinct from the physical. They are inner *worlds* of I-activity: when we deal with

events in thought, imagination, or memory, we may be concerned with the self and the other of relational perspectives, with
our bodily sensations and activities, or with actual occurrences.

The external world as the nonself comprises the aspects of
our experiencing that we ascribe to the (human and nonhuman)
other of our self–world engagements. It is not isomorphic with
the nonmental world of bodily sensation and action or of that
which is thought about. Our bodily experiences and motor
actions are our own, not external in the same way that another's
are. That which is thought about might be an aspect of ourselves
(the twinge in my tooth; the way I am dancing) or not (the
weather; a political issue).

The place of the dynamic and representational in our inner
and outer worlds is also in need of clarification. Classical conceptions suggest that the *Ich* (ego) is a dynamic (inner) world of
thought and trial action, whereas the external world comprises
the actual objects and events of the nonself world, registered
mentally as object representations. In ego-psychological perspectives, both self and the objects of the external world are representations; the ego is an organization of impersonal forces. Object
relations perspectives formally conceive of both the inner world
of the self and the external world of the other as representations,
although implicitly, in the active relations of self and other to one
another, they seem also to have a dynamic character.

We have by no means fully delineated developments (and
developmental failures) on the path from our earliest ways of
selving toward the formation of our internal and external
worlds. Clinical observation of transitions from id to ego, from
part-self and object relationships to whole-object ones, and from
paranoid-schizoid to depressive experience modes provides us
with rich sources from which to work toward clarification.
When a woman accepts as her own the feelings that underlie an
ego-alien urge to kill her child, can we say that she is enlarging
her internal world? In what sense might an abuse survivor be
expanding her internal and external worlds when she articulates her own and the other's parts in her dissociated abuse

constellations? Does the hypothetical patient of chapter 2 enlarge his internal and external worlds in both the self–other and mental–physical senses as he integrates his contrary scornful and idealizing feelings toward his colleague, his friend of adolescence, and his therapist?

An expanding body of infancy research is also yielding evidence for a wide variety of relevant early infant capacities that must ultimately be included in any full account of the ways we become capable of a sense of I-ness and how that capacity is reflected in our inner and outer worlds. Among the most immediately interesting are empirical data and hypotheses concerning early intentionality (Demos, 1992), patterns of attachment (Goldberg et al. 1995; Karen, 1994), microanalyses of infant–mother interactions (Beebe et al., 1997), developments that eventuate in capacities to use the self referential I (Lewis and Brooks-Gunn, 1979), the organization of early experience, memory, and language (Nelson, 1986), and the development of the subjective self (Stern, 1994)

We are in the early stages of identifying issues relevant to our notions of our internal and external worlds and beginning to resolve them. Here we focus on their self–nonself and mental–physical dimensions from the I-self perspective. We build on the notion that infants initially represent their self–world engagements in discrete perceptual-cognitive-affective-motor I-schemes in which the self and nonself and the mental and physical are not differentiated (schemes of nursing, visual tracking, and grasping; comfortable and uncomfortable holding situations). These agentic schemes are our earliest forms of selving, our primitive ways of interpreting events. They carry no subjective sense of I-ness or of an internal or external world.

self development occurs through the integration and differentiation of these schemes. Piaget's (Flavell, 1963) and Winnicott's (1971) paradigmatic examples (infants integrating their grasp and visual tracking schemes, their comfortable and uncomfortable infant–mother interactions) serve as models for I-self conceptions of integration and differentiation.

In integration processes, people establish the complexly lay-ered webs of I-schemes that constitute their dynamic selves, and, gradually, a sense of I-ness in their ways of perceiving, thinking, feeling, and acting. When the infant of Winnicott's example integrates its positive and negative feelings, both are modulated and, together, permit the infant more nuanced encodings of its affective interactions with others. With that integration, the infant makes a small advance toward experienc-ing its feelings in the first person. When Piaget's infant inte-grates its grasp and vision schemes, they become more flexibly available to the baby in its newly expanded modes of self–world engagement, and the infant increases its as yet rudimentary sense of I-ness in its motor activities.

As we grow up, we achieve a heightened sense of our own identities, of ourselves as the authors of our thoughts and actions. A sense of I-ness may now permeate the ways we encode events, perhaps in the oral and anal patterns that Freud drew to our attention; the schemes of having lunch at nursery school or going to the zoo that Nelson (1986) explores; the metaphoric projections of bodily activities, such as balancing, that in Johnson's (1987) conception form the templates by which we understand a person's emotional balance or the requirements of justice; or the internal working models that Fonagy and his colleagues (1993) explore to describe intergenerational patterns of child–parent relationships.

Every integration of schemes also results in the differentia-tion of their self and nonself aspects. In Winnicott's and Piaget's examples, the integration of comfortable and uncomfortable infant–mother interactions also results in the infant's beginning recognition of itself and its mother as distinct from one another; in the integration of grasping and vision schemes, the complex developments toward object permanence (the ring as external object), and of a coordinately stable, permanent self, also begin. In the self–other meaning of the terms internal and external, the infant is beginning to establish its inner and outer worlds as dis-tinct from one another.

In explorations of such schemes of understanding as meta-phoric projections, Internal Working Models, Nelson's event schemes, and Freud's oral and anal experience modes, questions of self–other differentiation have hardly arisen. The I-self concept suggests that, in every integration of such schemes into constellations by which we usefully make meaning of events, we also differentiate their self and nonself aspects, and, with those differentiations, we enlarge our internal and external worlds. Might we expect that, when our anal ways of understanding things become integral parts of our larger character orientations, we also more fully take into account our own and a partner's distinct ways of being tidy and untidy? As a young boy establishes increasingly complex ways of encoding lunch-at-nursery-school, will he also be more and more able to recognize a teacher's or a peer's food preferences as valid aspects of that person, although different from his own? Can we understand the correlation between a woman's reflective capacity and her ability to help her child toward secure attachment, as a result of her integrating remembered experiences with present understandings and, in the process, increasingly seeing both her mother and her own child as beings independent of herself, with their own capacities and difficulties? If we can usefully anticipate these self–other differentiations, can we then validly argue that in these activities people are enlarging their internal worlds of self (their own ways of being tidy, enjoying food, raising children) and their external ones (the ways of others), and that with this expansion their sense of I-ness in these activities is enlarged?

Every integration and differentiation of I-schemes also results in an increasing differentiation of the mental from the bodily aspects of activities and from the environmental events in which they are activated. When the infant of Winnicott's (1971) example integrates the perceptual-cognitive-affective-bodily I-schemes of its comfortable and uncomfortable infant–mother interactions, for example, the contrasting bodily experiences specific to the two schemes cannot become fully parts of the newly expanded and modulated feeling constellation. To that small extent the infant's feelings are freed from their absolute tie to their bodily concomitants. Similarly, when Piaget's infant integrates its grasping and vision schemes and can grasp the ring it sees, the bodily components specific to its grasping and visual tracking schemes cannot totally become aspects of the new seeing-grasping skill. The absolute body–mind unity of grasping and seeing begins to give way to the possibility of seeing and grasping mentally, independent of physical action and the physical presence of the relevant environmental objects. The infant is moving toward the establishment of the mental–physical dimension of its internal and external worlds, an intrapsychic world of feeling, thought, and trial action that carries a sense of I-ness distinct from the external world of physical sensation, the objects of thought, and motor action.[1]

As the mental aspects of I-schemes become free of their bodily components and of particular environmental events, they become flexibly available for such I-activities as symbolic play, remembering, and imagining. Now grasping may begin to refer not only to particular physical actions but to a person's way of being greedy for money; one might see the point of an argument independent of any visual activity. A child might remember a lunch-at-nursery-school event and tell his daddy about it or evoke it in imaginative play. A woman, herself insecurely attached, might be able to recapture in memory and rethink her earlier painful relations with her mother, without enacting them with her daughter. Balance, now more than an I-scheme activated in standing upright, can become a template for understanding emotional states, issues of justice, or the weight of argument. An internal world of mental selving is being formed: a sense of oneself as creator of one's thinking, feeling, remembering, and imagining.

Finally, in this conception, dynamic and representational organizations are not differentially ascribed to our internal or

---

[1] Fonagy and Target (Fonagy, 1995; Fonagy and Target, 1996; Target and Fonagy, 1996) have recently begun valuable elaborations of theoretical, clinical, and empirical perspectives on the development of capacities for "mentalizing" in children, and their relationships to the development of self.

our external worlds. Rather, representations of both self and nonself are constructed by dynamic schemes. With the integration of positive and negative infant–mother interactions, the infant's self representations and its representations of the mother, previously of a good self and good mother in one interaction, a bad self and a bad mother in the other, become a more complex representation of a self, both good and bad, and, equally, an ambivalent representation of the mother. The ring of Piaget's example, no more than a graspable in one scheme and a seeable in the other, becomes a graspable-seeable; the infant self, coordinately, becomes a grasper-see-er.

Throughout life, all representations, whether of self, other people, or the nonhuman world, occurring in present observation, memory, anticipations of the future, or dreams, reflect the I-scheme constellations that are active at the moment. For the young child of chapter 2, depending on the motivations then active, a ring might be the graspable of Piaget's example, or perhaps a circle for ring-around-the-rosie, a hoop, a halo around the moon, or a marriage signifier. The grieving man's self representations might include views of himself, at different moments, as utterly desolate, a playboy suddenly free, a zombie dead to all that is good, or a computer brain with no need for sentiment.

This conception of our inner and outer worlds suggests that we achieve a full sense of I-ness in our selving activities to the extent that our inner worlds are integrated constellations of I-schemes whose self and nonself aspects are differentiated, and whose mental aspects can be activated independently of their bodily ones and in the absence of the actual occurrences to which they refer. At every level of integration and differentiation, our me-selves (self representations) reflect the dynamic I-schemes being activated.

This dynamic and representational "innerness" of our self experience stands in contrast to the "outerness," in the self– other dimension, of those aspects of our I-schemes and their coordinate representations that we attribute to other persons and the impersonal world and, in the mental–physical dimension, to the "outerness" of that which is not intrapsychic (the objects of thought).

Toward an Internal World

In this I-self view, we experience our sense of I-ness as an inner world that is constituted and enlarged throughout our lives as we integrate I-schemes into increasingly complex networks. It is a perspective distinct in a number of ways from familiar psychoanalytic conceptions. Here we consider only a few of its implications to suggest its possible usefulness for our understanding of the self–other and the mental–physical dimensions of our internal worlds.

The Self–Other Dimension

In the I-self view, the self–other aspect of internality–externality is not the customary one, in which the self aspects of self–other units are seen as the internal world, the "other" aspects as the external, nonself one. Instead, people's internal worlds are identified with their I-scheme constellations as a whole. Our inner worlds are our ways of selving, of making meaning of events perceptually, emotionally, cognitively, or motorically. They carry our sense of I-ness.

Self and nonself are differentiated *within* them. In their selving activities, people might variously bring the self or nonself aspects of their I-schemes to the fore, depending on their current purposes. Throughout, however, a self or object aspect comes into consideration not as one part of a self–other unit but in the larger context of a particular meaning-making activity, the individual's "current purposes." A woman's internal working model of child–parent relationships, for example, may have led to her own insecure attachment. Now it is a constituent of her I-self (her inner world): it patterns her way of selving in her inter-actions with her own child. Gradually, perhaps with help, she becomes aware of various self and nonself aspects of this inter-action mode. She is modifying her inner world of I-activity, her ways of understanding child–parent relationships.

The woman of Loewald's illustration explores the relations to her husband and father that have contributed to her compulsion to kill her child. In this inner-world activity she might at various moments consider her own part in them, or her husband's or father's. In the I-self view, however, her "self" and the "others" (her husband and father) are not sense-based representations joined in self–other units. She can think meaningfully about her own part and theirs in her interactions with them only in the context of their place in her various relationships to them. It is within these I-scheme constellations that self and others have meaning for her. It is within them that she might differentiate her own and her husband's or father's parts in their relation-ships in new and more useful ways.

A girl who has moved from an urge to binge to a sense of eating in her own particular way might have little remaining need to focus on either the self or the nonself aspects of her ways of feeling hunger, stocking her larder, preparing food, or eating a meal. The result, however, is not a reduction in her sense of I-ness in these activities. On the contrary, as these ways of feeling and acting become integrated aspects of her personal ways of going about things, her sense of agency and I-ness in them is enhanced, although their self and nonself aspects may have largely retreated to the background.

The Mental–Physical Dimension

Questions of Internalization. The relation of the mental and phys-ical to our internal and external worlds takes a form different from the one widely accepted in psychoanalytic thought. The notion that our internal worlds are arenas of self aware mental activity is widely accepted. However, the I-self idea that our ways of selving intrapsychically are products of differentiation may seem quite foreign.

Even Loewald (1979), altogether committed to the notion that our internal and external worlds are differentiation products, focuses exclusively on self–other differentiation in their establishment. He does not view the mental–physical aspects of our internal and external worlds as resulting from the differentiation of the mental and physical aspects of our initially global, perceptual-cognitive-affective relationship units. Rather, in familiar psychoanalytic terms, he suggests that environmental self–world interactions become aspects of our psychic structures as we "internalize" them. In these processes of internalization, they are "transposed to a new arena, thus becoming intrapsychic interactions" (p. 211). It is these intrapsychic interactions that carry a sense of I-ness.

The phenomena identified as internalizations are familiar enough. The internalization of the superego might be exemplified by a young girl's feeling conscience stricken in ways patterned in her interactions with her father, although she is not now in his presence and he knows nothing of her current misdeed. The man in Freud's example might *recall* his early defiant and critical behavior toward his parents' authority, rather than *enacting* it in relation to the analyst. A woman, having reexamined her internal working model of child–mother interactions, might be able to hold them in memory without repeating them in her interactions with her own child. In a trial action, a person might play out imaginatively a prospective dinner at a restaurant before making a reservation.

To understand these mental activities as products of internalization, however, raises unanswered (and probably unanswerable) questions. It seems to suggest that when our selving activities occur in the environment they are somehow mind free, although a man's overbearing actions toward his analyst are surely not without mental content; and, when a woman expresses a long-established internal working model in her engagement with her child, her enactment is both mental and physical.

It is altogether unclear, moreover, how one might imagine the processes by which such environmental interactions could be "transposed" into psychic ones. And, finally, the notion of transposition seems to imply that, when an internalization has occurred, the interaction, previously environmental and now internal, has left the external world and is no longer active there, although that implication is clearly unintended.

In the differentiation perspective, the mental and the physical are not distinct and alternate forms of experience; the mental does not replace the bodily or environmental in a form of transposition. Rather, the mental and physical are initially undifferentiated aspects of our perceptual-affective-cognitive-motor schemes. When we have differentiated their mental and physical aspects, our selving possibilities are expanded; we can think and feel and act mentally *with or without* the associated bodily sensations and environmental activities.[2]

Our intrapsychic trial actions, when we have largely achieved mental–physical distinctions, may or may not eventuate in environmental action. A woman's internal working model, rooted in her own past child–mother interactions, might be readily avail-

---

[2] This alternative way of framing the observations that have been traditionally included in the conception of internalization has implications for notions of introjection and identification too complex for thorough exploration here. In such a discussion, an introject could not be seen the traditional way as an internalized part-object that may in various ways attack, reproach, or approve of the individual, an identification as an assimilated (internalized) aspect or property of another. Introjection would, instead, be explored as a relatively isolated I-scheme constellation whose (part) self and (part) other aspects are incompletely articulated. Related introjection–projection processes might be examined as aspects of the easy reversal of self and nonself in isolated I-scheme constellations. Examinations of introjection in these terms must also include the place of other aspects of experience that we expect to find in such isolated I-scheme constellations (those suggested in chapters 4 and 5), aspects perhaps accounting for observations of "incorporation" or people's sense of an introject as a foreign body somehow inside them. The integration of I-schemes and the resulting dynamic networks of I-schemes and their coordinate representations might be explored, then, to examine how well they might accommodate the large body of work dealing with identification.

able to memory but with only limited and largely controlled expression in her ways of raising her own child. One's remembered defiance toward one's parents might be experienced only mentally and reported to one's analyst, be enacted in the therapeutic hour in a temporary dedifferentiation of their mental and physical aspects, and, perhaps in response to interpretation, be once more evoked psychically, independently of any interpersonal expression.

A sense of I-ness occurs not only when actions are exclusively intrapsychic. Our activities, whether only intrapsychic or also expressed environmentally, carry a firm sense of I-ness if we have established the mental–physical differentiations that permit us to act mentally with or without physical action. A man might have a clear sense of I-ness in making a restaurant reservation he has first anticipated mentally. A woman might have a vivid sense of her personal aliveness as she becomes able to raise her child in her own way rather than in accord with patterns established in her own childhood. It is when mental–physical differentiation is lacking, when thought *cannot* occur independently of action, that environmental actions become enactments with at most a rudimentary sense of I-ness.

Constructing the Mental and Physical Dimensions of Experience. The idea that the mental and physical aspects of our selving activities are differentiation products raises other interesting problems. It invites the possibility that, when we differentiate the mental and physical aspects of our global I-schemes, we are not only differentiating the mental from the physical and becoming able to act mentally, we are both constructing the intrapsychic ways of selving of our internal worlds and forming our notions of the physicality of our external worlds (of our bodies, other people and the nonhuman). If we observe incompleteness or disturbance in one differentiation component (e.g., our mental activities), we will find concomitant difficulties in the other (our understanding of our bodily sensations or our physical worlds).

And, to the extent that our differentiations of the mental and physical aspcts of our experiences are disturbed or incomplete, our sense of I-ness in those experiences will be lost.

In Davies and Frawley's (1994) observation, for example, the highly competent young attorney was unable to experience her anticipated business meeting with a senior partner of her firm without the bodily concomitants of vaginal sensation, trembling, and pallor, which could later be seen as evocations of earlier abuse experiences. The differentiation perspective would invite us to expect that, if this intrusion of the bodily into the relational-emotional-cognitive is common in such dissociated experiences, we will also observe intrusions of relational aspects of interactions on bodily experience. And, indeed, Davies and Frawley observe that bodily symptoms later understood to be concomitants of early abusive relationships are so often taken by patients and physicians to represent actual bodily dysfunctions that patients frequently have histories replete with undiagnosable illnesses, hospitalizations, and invasive but inconclusive medical procedures.

The larger body of Davies and Frawley's work, moreover, encourages the inference that it is when these dissociated abuse relationships are increasingly integrated into the larger networks of patients' experience that their emotional aspects can increasingly occur without inappropriate bodily concomitants, and conversely, bodily experience can reliably be attributed to actual bodily occurrences. It is in the course of this integration and the associated mental–physical differentiation that we might expect patients' feelings of I-ness to grow, their abilities to have a sense of personal authorship of both their memories and their bodily experiences as integral parts of their own lives.

Might we expect, similarly, that when a man cannot relinquish an unrealistic feeling of guilt for his father's death, he might also have difficulty recognizing that his actual behaviors have only limited consequences? Can we anticipate that if he is able to diminish his guilt feelings by recognizing that he was helpless in the face of his father's death, will he also have a clearer sense of his own physical capacities and limitations? And will he then also have a greater sense of I-ness in both his mental and his physical activities?

Would it be valid to anticipate that if a girl experiences the disappointment of a low examination grade in an unshakable sense of "I'm fat!" she might also have difficulty interpreting actual bodily experiences accurately (a tickle in her throat as only the onset of a cold; stomach sensations as no more than a need to eat)? And might we expect, as the I-self concept suggests, that, as she becomes better able to differentiate accurately the mental and physical, she will also have a stronger sense of having an inner world and a more vivid sense of herself as the author of her thoughts and agent of her self–world engagements?

My patient Gary, in his gallant efforts to understand himself and his world, provides us with what seems to have been an at least momentary success at differentiating the mental-emotional from the literal-physical. Typically, when Gary spoke of his ghost feelings, he seemed to take his sense of himself as ghostly quite literally, particularly at night, when it also seemed to him that the dark was peopled by ghosts. On one triumphant occasion, when he was talking again about ghost feelings, he emphasized with obvious joy, "Not ghosts . . . ghost feelings." For the moment, at least, he was able to differentiate the metaphoric from the literal; he could experience ghost feelings without the conviction that he or others were literally ghosts. Can we speculate, as the I-self conception hypothesizes, that, when Gary was able to experience ghost *feelings*, he might also have experienced the external world as more solidly substantial? And can we expect, further, that when he was successfully making this mental–physical distinction, he had a little more sense than before of his own I-ness in his feelings and actions?

Searles's (1962) illuminating observations of schizophrenic experience modes, and a supporting examination of Rorschach imagery in a nonclinical group (Fast, 1969), suggest experiences not unlike Gary's. In the traditional view (e.g., Goldstein, 1944; Hanfmann and Kasanin, 1952) concrete thought is rooted in the external world of immediate sense perception and precedes the symbolic thought of our internal worlds developmentally. In familiar psychoanalytic terms, we gradually internalize our concrete-literal ways of experiencing to form our inner worlds. In disorders such as schizophrenia and brain damage, the person's capacity for thinking abstractly is impaired. To the extent that abstract thinking is undeveloped or disturbed, the person thinks concretely.

Searles's clinical observations of schizophrenic experience convinced him that this view cannot be sustained. It seemed to him, on the contrary, that, in ways congruent with the I-self conception, the capacities for thinking concretely and abstractly (e.g., in metaphor) are established *together* in processes of differentiation. In schizophrenic deterioration, that differentiation is lost and, in recovery, is established again. Moreover, he argues that one's sense of identity (the sense of I-ness in one's activities) is closely associated with the achievement or reachievement of the capacity for both figurative thought and an appreciation of the world in all its substantial physicality.

Searles notes, as others have done, that his schizophrenic patients are unable to think metaphorically. A patient who spoke of feeling that he was "just nothing . . . like tissue paper" was not intending a metaphor or simile: on a windy day he was quite literally afraid that he might be blown away. The comment, "You can't have your cake and eat it too," might elicit a patient's furious assertion that he does not want to eat any cake in this hospital.

Searles observes, however, that this deterioration of symbolic thought does not lead to greater reliance on a concrete, sense-based reality. When patients are unable to think abstractly, they are equally unable to think in concrete terms, to perceive objects as literal, solid, stable wholes. A patient who cannot think abstractly might also "know" that an actual person is easily transformed into a person of a different sex, a sheep, or a piece of furniture. People and inanimate objects might seem, as they did to Gary, shadowy or ghostlike. The patient sensing himself to be no more than tissue paper might believe that he could literally be blown away by the wind.[3]

That is, Searles's observations suggested to him that we establish our internal (mental) worlds and our external (physical) worlds together in processes of differentiation and that with this differentiation we also achieve a sense of I-ness in our self–world engagements. The schizophrenic person's loss of capacities for abstract or symbolic thought is matched by an equal loss in the ability to appreciate the concrete reality of objects. And with that dedifferentiation the sense of I-ness in one's activities is lost.

In recovery, both the internal and external worlds are reconstituted: when a patient is able to perceive a piece of cake in all its physicality, he will also be able to understand the saying, "You can't have your cake and eat it too." If the man Searles describes, could sense his feeling like tissue paper as metaphoric, he would not need to fear that his actually substantial body could be blown away by the wind.[4]

Searles's hypothesis that we establish our capacities for abstract thought and for the appreciation of the physical world in processes of differentiation suggests the possibility that, in their construction of Rorschach images, people who ascribe physical characteristics to abstract ideas will, conversely, also

---

[3] Hanna Segal (1957) describes this nondifferentiation of symbol from what is symbolized as a symbolic equation. She describes a patient who was asked by his doctor why, since his illness (a schizophrenic breakdown), he had stopped playing the violin. He replied with some violence, "Why? Do you expect me to masturbate in public?" (p. 391). Segal suggests that prior to the patient's breakdown the violin functioned in a sublimated way as a symbol for his penis but that now a dedifferentiation had occurred: the violin no longer *represented* the penis but was *equated with* it.

In ways that strikingly anticipated the I-self conception, she has suggested that the capacity for symbolization proper occurs with developments in self–other differentiation and ego (self) integration. Moreover, she observes that, with the differentiation of symbol and symbolized, "there is a growing sense of reality both internal and external" (p. 394), a sense, as I understand it, of I-ness and of the substantial reality of the physical world.

[4] As adults it may be hard for us to imagine the occurrence of such instability in one's external world except in severe disturbance. Parents or other

construct images of objects that lack their appropriate physical characteristics.

That hypothesis was strongly supported in the Rorschach protocols of 135 college students who were not clinically involved patients. Students who attributed physical properties (form, color, or shading) to such abstract concepts as electricity, wind, "the spirits of two calves," or "the void of time" also tended to construct images of physical objects without the substantiality appropriate to them, "a chair, somebody sitting in it . . . reading a newspaper . . . a shadow . . . you can't see the person"; "a creature . . . lying on some sort of invisible plain"; "man . . . looks like you can see through him" (p. 332).

The Rorschach materials do not offer possibilities for exploring associations between the students' incomplete mental–physical differentiation and the quality of I-ness in their activities. Searles's (1962) clinically based view, like the I-self hypothesis, suggests that, to the extent that their mental–physical differentiations were incomplete, their sense of I-ness would also be compromised.

It is a view that Ogden (1986) strongly shares:

> One might well ask whether the sense of I-ness makes it possible to differentiate between symbol and symbolized or whether the differentiation of symbol and symbolized allows for the emergence of a sense of I-ness. I would view both as true: each makes the other possible, but neither is the cause of the other in a linear sense [p. 72].

Our studies of self integration (Fast et al., 1996), finally, hint at a way of exploring the I-self notion that mental–physical

---

observers of young children may have less difficulty in doing so. A young mother, for example, delightedly reported that she had been reading her daughter's favorite book, *Goodnight Moon*, with her, when she was called to the telephone. She put the book down on the bed. When she turned, she saw the little girl standing in the crib, intently focused on the open book and tentatively putting a foot on the page, evidently, as it seemed to her, considering that she might enter the pictured room.

differentiation is coordinate to self integration. We asked story-tellers to respond to a picture showing a man hanging by his hands from a branch and supporting a young boy on each foot. Their stories typically spoke of a father and his sons enjoying the outdoors together or of the boys' pleasure in their father's prowess. At the lowest level of self integration, however, and only at that level, we also observed apparent fusions of the metaphorical and the literal. Storytellers veered from speaking of the father's literal difficulty in holding on to the branch and supporting the boys perched on his feet to his being "out on a limb" in dealing with his family, his difficulty in "holding on" financially or in "supporting" the boys in their growing up; again, apparently without noticing, the storytellers reverted to literal meanings.

In this group of stories, those that showed very limited self integration were the only ones in which we observed confusion between the metaphoric and literal. It is not possible from these materials to determine which comes first, self integration or the differentiation of the metaphorical and the literal. Nor did we observe this relationship in a large enough group to evaluate its stability across groups. At most, the co-occurrence of low levels of self integration and incomplete differentiation of the metaphorical and literal suggests a direction for testing the hypothesis that, in the establishment of an integrated network of I-schemes that constitute the dynamic self, we also establish our inner worlds of mental activity free of bondage to the phys-ical. and of our physical worlds in all their substantiality.[5]

---

[5] The notion that the cognitive and affective-interpersonal are separate aspects of psychic structure and occur in distinct developmental lines is firmly entrenched in both academic and psychoanalytic psychologies. It may seem strange, in that context, to suggest that low levels of self integration may be related to failures in maintaining the (cognitive) distinction between the metaphorical and the literal. It is interesting, then, that Main (1991) reports analogous findings, specifically between children's attachment patterns and

Summary

In this chapter we have turned our attention from experience in which people have at most a rudimentary sense of I-ness to that in which they have a sense of their own active involvement in their ways of perceiving, thinking, feeling, and acting. They are engaged in the *Ich* (ego) activity of Freud's conception, the whole-object interactions of relational perspectives, and the depressive experience mode of Ogden's view

In these experience modes, people have a sense of themselves as living in an internal world of self distinct from the external, nonself world. Two disparate notions of internal and external are typically confused. On one hand, the internal world is taken to be the self; the external world, those aspects of our experience that we attribute to the nonself. On the other hand, the internal world is a world of mental activity in perception, thought, imagination, and memory distinct from the external world of physical action and the world of actual events.

In the I-self view, neither the self and nonself nor the mental and physical aspects of experience are differentiated in the global I-schemes of infancy. It is in the integration and differentiation of I-schemes that we establish our internal worlds of self as distinct from nonself and of intrapsychic activities distinct from the physical.

In this view, our internal worlds take a different form than in traditional perspectives. They are complexly layered constellations of I-schemes, the patterns by which we encode our experiences. They carry a sense of I-ness to the extent that we

---

their capacities for metacognition (thinking about thinking). These studies found, for example, that at age six, securely attached children more clearly recognize that thoughts are private than do insecurely attached children. Neither the storytellers' metaphoric–literal confusions nor those of the children in the attachment studies point to causal directions from one to the other. Rather, both the I-self and the attachment frameworks suggest intricate interweaving of cognitive and affective development throughout development.

differentiate their self and nonself, and their mental and physical aspects.

On the self–nonself dimension, our inner worlds are not the self aspects of self–other units. Dynamic I-schemes are primary: we bring their self and nonself aspects into focus as circumstances dictate.

The mental–physical aspects of our internal worlds are not composed of physical activities in some way internalized to become mental ones. They are products of differentiations that permit us to evoke the mental aspects of our ways of understanding events with or without the physical ones.

Our intrapsychic ways of thinking, feeling, and acting are not developmentally more advanced than our appreciation of substantial, nonmental realities of physical objects and actions. Rather, the mental and physical develop together by differentiation; we can appreciate matters mentally only to the extent that we are also able to apprehend their physical aspects. Our sense of I-ness is not limited to intrapsychic of "internalized" interactions. It informs our mental and our environmental activities to the extent that we have achieved self–other and mental–physical differentiations.

This view of our internal worlds implies a correspondingly different conception of our external world. A beginning exploration of some of its parameters is the subject of chapter 7.

7

FROM SELVING WITHOUT A SENSE OF I-NESS TO FIRST-PERSON EXPERIENCING——II

TOWARD AN EXTERNAL WORLD

The view of our internal worlds we began to explore in chapter 6 implies a markedly different "external" world than that of traditional psychoanalysis. In that objectivist perspective, the external world is the real world, accurately perceived by our senses and registered in our minds in object representations. It is a discovered world that exerts its influence from the time children "turn to reality" at about two years of age and begin to take its parameters into account. Along the self–nonself dimension, it is the external world of other people, which we take into account with increasing accuracy in developmental or clinical processes of introjection and projection. Along the mental–physical dimension, it is the world of reality that we come to symbolize in the establishment of our internal worlds. People's experiences of the external world may be distorted by personally motivated wishes, conflicts, and defenses originating in the drives. In the classical perspective, it is a central function of analysis to remove these drive-based distortions and give people back the true (sense-based) history of their lives.

In the I-self view, we construct our external worlds in our self–world engagements. Our discussion so far has focused on our external worlds as products of our self–other and mental–physical differentiations. They are *our* worlds, constituents of the I-schemes by which we understand and act on events. They may include an infant's way of encoding a ring as nothing but a see-able, a man's perception of a piece of cake in all its substantial physicality, or a woman's view of her daughter patterned by an old internal working model. There is, however, another aspect of our external worlds, the worlds *of which* we make meaning. The infant constructs its vision scheme as it tracks a physically present ring; a man builds a metaphor in his appreciation of the edible character of actual cake; the woman interacts with her daughter, a real child with all her complex actualities. These are the worlds independent of meaning-making activities.

We can call the first the created world, the second, the discovered one.[1] In all our activities—perceptual, cognitive, affective, and motor—we engage both the created worlds *by which* we make meaning, and the discovered worlds *of which* we make meaning. The children of Nelson's (1989) studies, for example, understood a second episode of fire drill (discovered world) in terms of the (created world) scheme established in their first one. Reciprocally, as they encountered variations in successive fire-drill events, they enlarged the established (created) world of their I-schemes to account more fully for these newly perceived (discovered world) parameters.

In this view, our created external worlds, although formed through our personally motivated activities, are by no means only distortions of reality; they are products of our ways of making meaning of events. Conversely our discovered worlds are not organizations of passively received, perception-based

---

[1] In a broader sense, our "discovered" worlds are also constructed, that is, unavailable to us in the form of pristine "objective reality." The heuristic differentiation proposed here, however, suffices for the present discussion.

registrations of an objective world; they are action products: aspects of actuality we include in our I-schemes as we discover them in our attempts to understand and act on events

We do not progress clinically or developmentally as we *diminish* the influence of personally motivated constructions of our external worlds in favor of an objective and undistorted apprehension of a discovered world. Quite the reverse. In development and clinical exploration, we *enlarge* our (created) ways of encoding events to take their actual (discovered) parameters into account in ever more complexly organized systems.

Our Created External Worlds

In this view we establish and enlarge our external worlds in our I-scheme integrations with their attendant self–other and mental–physical differentiations. We anticipate that if Gary could have reliably differentiated the mental and literal aspects of his ghost experiences as "ghost feelings . . . not ghosts," his external world would have achieved increasing substantiality. If a woman, herself insecurely attached, comes to differentiate her own and her mother's ways of behaving in their mother–child relationship, she will achieve a greater sense of the externality of her mother and the independent, "external" reality of her child. If Searles's (1962) patient could have understood his sense that he was like tissue paper as metaphoric rather than literal, he might also more securely have experienced the full physicality of his actual body.

These external worlds are fundamentally dynamic worlds rather than Freud's exclusively representational ones. In the differentiation of our I-schemes, we attribute both to other people, and to the impersonal world, feelings, thoughts, and actions in relation to our sense of ourselves and our own thinking, feeling, and acting. Our external worlds of people are worlds of other subjects: of abusive others with their personally motivated intentions and actions; of one's mother and one's own child, each with her own ways of going at things. They are the intersubjective worlds that have been the focus of Benjamin's (1988, 1995) clinical explorations and of Stern's (1985) inventive studies of cross-modal attunements in late infancy.

Our nonpersonal worlds are no less dynamic, although they are worlds of impersonal forces rather than human intentions and feelings. In the course of self–nonself and mental–physical differentiation, we gradually learn to attribute personal actions to ourselves and other people, and impersonal ones to the nonhuman—the wind as not trying to blow our hats off, the sun as not actively working to warm us, the rain on our parade as not an intended frustration.

Our created worlds are also representational. They are not worlds of sensory input accurately registered in the mind, but representations structured by dynamic schemes. For the infant, the ring of Piaget's paradigmatic example is a graspable only in one I-scheme and a seeable in the other. The mother in Winnicott's (1971) example is either a good mother or a bad mother for the infant, depending on the affective-cognitive-action schemes then in play.

With every integration of schemes, our representations of people and objects become more stable, less vulnerable to erratic changes in meaning with every shift in mood, activity, or wish. By about age two we have established an initial object constancy, a representational world,[2] although, as Fraiberg (1969) reminds us, our libidinal object constancy at age two may be only rudimentary.

As we work out our sense of our own identities in further (dynamic) development, we acquire the ability to represent our "external" mothers variously as the Earth Mother of generous

---

[2] This view of the external world has roots in Sandler and Rosenblatt's (1962) proposition the we construct our external worlds rather than receiving them passively as sensory registrations, and Loewald's (1980) view that we construct them in processes of self–other differentiation.

giving, the destructive witch of our envious furies, the friend of our adulthood, or the increasingly frail object of our concern. A woman's representations of her abuser may be structured and restructured as she integrates the myriad dynamic I-schemes that originate in the early abusive interactions. A ring, initially only a seeable and a graspable, may, in our later (dynamic) activities be represented as a member of the class of circular objects, subject to formulae that define its circumference and area or, in metaphoric projections, useful in thinking about the cycle of seasons or a song cycle.

These dynamic and representational external worlds are, in a significant sense, created worlds. Their structure depends on the ways we have integrated and differentiated the initially global I-schemes that represent our self–world engagements. They are products of our ways of making meaning.

Our Discovered External Worlds

To say that we discover our worlds as well as creating them implies that we do not make meaning out of whole cloth: we make meaning of actual occurrences. When, as Stern (1994) describes, a young child establishes particular relational patterns in its interactions with its depressed mother it does so in efforts to reanimate the mother whose responsiveness is genuinely impaired. As Eagle (1984a) emphasizes in sharp disagreement with Spence (1982), when clinicians work with patients to construct meaningful accounts of their lives, they do not ignore the actualities being accounted for, histories of abuse, for example, or personal losses in the Holocaust.

We discover aspects of these "actual" worlds as our established (created) ways of encoding events prove insufficient to accommodate our present circumstances. An infant, acting in terms of its established nursing scheme, fails to find the nipple. An adult victim of childhood abuse, remembering an uncle who was always generous with small change for ice cream and candy, feels an inexplicable panic. A girl, already proficient at computing the area of squares and rectangles, is stymied by circles. It is in resolving these disjunctions that we discover more about our actual worlds—an enlarged arena in which the nipple may be found, unacceptable abusiveness in one's generous uncle, a way of computing the area of circles.

Our Created and Discovered Worlds in Our Selving Activities

In traditional psychoanalytic perspectives, the objective (discovered) external world is the criterion for reality. Personal motivations (loosely, created worlds), rooted in the drives, distort our experience of reality. In the course of development and clinical work we try to remove these distortions and live in terms of the actualities of the "real," objective world.

The I-self perspective invites us to consider a different notion of relationships between our created and discovered worlds. On one hand, in this view the created external world of our I-scheme constellations is not merely a consequence of distortion but, rather, is forged in our active and adaptive engagements with our worlds. On the other hand, although in a significant sense we create our external worlds, we do not create them out of whole cloth. We also attend to the "discovered" worlds of actual events.

Our aim, then, cannot be to remove the influence of our created worlds in favor of an accurate apprehension of objective reality. Nor can it be, as radical constructivists, such as Spence (1982) suggest, to ignore the actualities of our experience since we cannot divine their objective reality in any case. On the contrary, the notion that both the created worlds of our I-scheme constellations and the world of actual (discovered) events are valid and important aspects of our activities invites explorations of how we might usefully think about their relations in our self–world engagements.[3]

Piaget's conceptions of assimilation and accommodation are congruent in major ways with these notions of our created and discovered worlds. In processes of assimilation, we understand a (discovered world) event in terms of our established (created world) schemes; in accommodation we modify our (created world) interpretations in light of (discovered world) actualities. In Piaget's view, as in the I-self perspective, the two processes interact in every activity from the beginning of life. In early development, in Piaget's view as in the I-self conception, infants do not differentiate the two. For example, an infant, enacting its (created world) nursing scheme might first fail to find, and then find, the (discovered world) nipple As observers, we might understand that the infant has modified its nursing scheme to accommodate new aspects of its (discovered) world. The infant itself, however, does not differentiate the created world of its I-scheme constellation from the (discovered world) actuality it now takes into account. It does not differentiate the created world *by which* it makes meaning of the nursing event, from the nursing event *of which* it makes meaning. As Flavell (1963) emphasizes, assimilation and accommodation occur as a single, indivisible experience.

From his psychoanalytic perspective, Ogden (1986) illuminates the ways this nondifferentiation might be echoed in adulthood and contrasts it with experience in which interpretation and actuality are more fully differentiated. He observes that, in the nondifferentiated paranoid-schizoid mode, people have no sense that they are interpreting their experience. They are trapped in the manifest: it seems to them that events speak for themselves. In Piagetian terms, a person who does not differentiate his interpretations from

---

[3] Benjamin (1995) usefully draws attention to a tendency in psychoanalytic thinking to elide the distinction between "real" others and their internal representations, in favor of only the mental representation (of whole- or part-objects or as selfobjects). Her corrective emphasis on the need to take both into account is consonant with the view presented here.

the actuality "sees the world from a single point of view only—his own—but without knowledge of the existence of other viewpoints or perspectives, and . . . without awareness that he is the prisoner of his own" (Flavell, 1963, p. 60).

In the depressive mode, by contrast, people distinguish their interpretations of events from the event itself. They have a sense of mediating between their thoughts and what is thought about. Now, Ogden (1986) argues, an event is what one makes of it; its significance lies in the interpretation one gives it. In I-self terms, people can now take into account differentially both the created (interpreted) and discovered (actual) aspects of their external worlds in their activities. They can consider an event from various perspectives to find the one most useful in a particular circumstance.

Piagetian theory also introduces the notion of balance between our creating and discovering activities in our self–world engagements. In all our activities we optimally achieve

> a kind of balance, a functional state in which . . . naively realistic[4] accommodations to reality are effectively held in check by assimilatory processes which can organize and direct accommodations, and in which assimilation. is kept from being riotously autistic by a sufficiency of continuing accommodatory adjustments to the real world [Flavell, 1963, 1965].

Piaget suggested that this balance varies from activity to activity. At one extreme, in pretend play or daydreaming, assimilation properly dominates: a broomstick can be a horse; a bicycle can be an Indy 500 racer. At the other extreme, in scientific work or preparing a budget, accommodation is fundamental: we work to modify scientific hypotheses in the light of experi-

---

[4] Flavell is referring here to naive realism in the epistemological sense. It is not that people attend only to the actualities of an event. Rather, as in Ogden's paranoid-schizoid mode, they might observably interpret it in a particular way, but they themselves have no sense that they are interpreting; for them, the event is what it is, a manifest actuality.

mental events; the actualities of our financial situation are central to our budget preparations.

Such a view might find experience in the paranoid-schizoid mode to represent an imbalance toward naive realism, people's loss of any sense that they are interpreting their experience, and with it an inability to examine a matter from various perspectives, or to imagine a point of view other than their own. In the other direction of imbalance, my patient Gary might seem to have been thinking in a "riotously autistic" way when he anticipated that he would have his Parents' Visit if the Emersons came from his home town at the usual time and the visit occurred in the usual place. He does not sufficiently take into account the actuality that the Emersons were not his parents and that, however fervently he interpreted the situation as a Parents' Visit, in actuality no Parents' Visit could occur.

Traditional psychoanalytic psychology hardly permits the notion of balance between interpretation and actuality to arise: the interpretation-free external world is king; personally motivated (drive based) interpretations are distortions to be removed.[5] Nevertheless, the exigencies of clinical work have created some consideration of the issue, most focally in the interpretation of people's responses to the Rorschach inkblots. The blots themselves are (discovered world) actualities of which meaning is to be made; clinical interest focuses on the (created world) mental patterns by which people make meaning of them.

In their classic monograph, Rapaport, Gill, and Schafer (1946) explored the balance that people achieve between inter-

---

[5] It may be this conception of the internal and external world that led Winnicott (1971) to propose the notion of transitional states, a third realm beween solipsistic subjectivity and objective perception. It is the realm of play and imagination, in which we move between the pole of altogether subjective experiencing and that of interpretation-free engagement of objective reality. The I-self notion that in *every* activity we find a balance between creating and discovering activities suggests that this "third realm" might be seen as encompassing *all* our ways of going about things, the appropriate balance shifting toward one or the other pole (in daydream as opposed to budget making) but probably never reaching the extreme of either.

pretation and actuality in their construction of Rorschach images. The authors did so in traditional terms, as a matter of relations between perception (the mental registration of objective reality) and association (interpretive thought). In their concept of "distance" between perception and association, they suggested an optimum distance in which interpretation and perception play appropriate parts in the person's response, too great and too little distance being reflections of particular forms of disturbance.

It is widely accepted that attention to how people integrate the actualities of the blots and their interpretations of them is clinically useful. The distance concept itself, however, has been troublesome. It implies that some forms of disturbance center in individuals' excessive distance from reality, others in loss of distance. But, in ways not easy to account for in this view, a single individual's responses might alternately show too great a distance from the actuality and loss of distance. Even worse, the same response might simultaneously show both too great a distance from the acuality and loss of distance from it.

The notion of balance between creative and discovering activities (assimilation and accommodation) suggests, rather, that when people have incompletely differentiated the two processes, they are likely to lose balance in *both* directions. In their construction of Rorschach images, they will both overweight the interpretive in relation to the actualities of the blot *and* overemphasize the actualities of the blot at the expense of their interpretive activities. In Rapaport et al.'s "distance" terms, too great a distance and loss of distance will occur together: people who, at one moment, too greatly emphasize the interpretive aspects in their responding to the neglect of the actualities of the blot will, at another moment, overemphasize blot actualities and fail to recognize their own interpretive activity.

To explore this possibility, 50 protocols of adult outpatients were examined for evidence that loss of balance in patients' sense of their interpretive (created world) activity in their construction of Rorschach images would be correlated with loss of

balance in their attention to the blots' (discovered world) actualities (Young and Fast, 1985). Too great an emphasis on the interpretive (assimilative) aspect of their responding was scored
when patients did not attempt to justify their responses by reference to the (discovered world) blot characteristics, whether or
not that justification could have been successful. When asked to
do so, (What about the blot made it look that way?) they might
say, "I just said that because I was thinking of it"; "It's on my
mind because of a biology lecture I heard yesterday"; or "I didn't
really see it. . . . It was just the association."

Too great an emphasis on the actuality of the blots (overac-
commodation) was scored when patients took their interpretations as recognitions of actualities rather than as interpretations
of an ambiguous stimulus. They might treat the blot as a puzzle
with an inherent meaning, and they might try to "figure out"
what a blot represented. They might express uncertainty about
their response being right or wrong. They might try to find
"intended" connections among blot areas. In more complicated
fusions of interpretation and actuality, a patient might justify
one interpretation, ("a flower") by reference to another blot area
taken as an actuality (What makes it look like a flower? "The
petals") and, again, take their first flower interpretation as an
actuality that justifies the second, petals. (What makes it look
like petals? "What else would a flower have?")

Patients did not consistently respond in ways that suggested
either too great a distance from the blot or loss of distance.
Instead, congruent with the differentiation view, patients who,
at one moment, elaborated their associations with little attention to the actual blot characteristics ("I just thought that"; It
was just "an association"), tended also, at other moments, to
focus exclusively on the "factual" characteristics of the blot and
were oblivious of their interpretive activity (the flower as an
actuality that justifies the "petals" response). That is, when
patients interpreting the Rorschach inkblots did not find an
appropriate balance between their interpretive (created world)
activity and taking into account the (discovered world) actuali-

ties of the inkblots, they tended to overbalance in both directions: failing at one moment to attend sufficiently to the blot
actuality and, at another, failing to recognize their interpretive
activity.[6]

Summary

The I-self conception of our internal worlds gives rise to a view
of our external worlds different from the traditional one. In I-
self view, our external worlds have two aspects, the created
world of the I-schemes *by which* we make meaning of events,
and the discovered world *of which* we make meaning.

We construct our created worlds through processes of
self–other and mental–physical differentiation. They are products of our engagements with actual events and are continuously
modified to take "discovered world" parameters more fully into
account. Both dynamic and representational, they include those
aspects of our I-schemes that we attribute to other people (their
ways of feeling, thinking, and acting) and the impersonal world
of causal forces and the representations that stand for them.
They are in significant ways *our* external worlds: products of our
ways of understanding our self–world engagements.

Our discovered worlds are the worlds of actuality independent of our meaning-making activities. We discover new aspects
of their parameters when our ways of making meaning fail to
account for events (the baby does not find the nipple; ways of
computing the area of squares do not apply to circles; the thought
of a generous uncle gives rise to panic). In every self–world
engagement both the created and the disavowed worlds play a

---

[6] In the earlier publication of this material (Young and Fast, 1985) Linda
Young and I framed the problem as one of coordinate failures in developments
beyond primary creativity (too fully accepting one's interpretations as reality)
and omnipotence (inability to recognize that the inkblots are products of
impersonal causality rather than personal intention.

part. In early development, and in the relatively unintegrated experience of adulthood, the creating and discovering aspects of our external worlds are not differentiated. In Ogden's and Piaget's very similar terms a "naive realism" prevails; unable to recognize their own interpretive activity distinct from the actuality they are interpreting, people take their experience for reality.

The goal of development and of clinical work is not the removal of our personally motivated (created world) interpretations from our experience in favor of a sense-based, objective (discovered) reality. Rather, in optimum development we achieve a balance between them, appropriate to the circumstances at hand: from the predominance of "creating" (assimilation) in symbolic play or daydreaming at one extreme to that of "discovering" (accommodation) at the other, perhaps in scientific endeavor or dealing with financial matters. In less optimum functioning, we might observe an imbalance: in their Rorschach responses, for example, people may fluctuate between inappropriately weighting their interpreting activity to the neglect of the blot actualities and focus on the blot actualities without recogniting their interpretive activity.

8 WHAT SORT OF A SELF IS THIS DYNAMIC I-SELF?

An I-Self of Selving: A Me-Self of Self Representations

Our I-selves are dynamic, but they are not selves that do things, selves that remember, interpret events, imagine, work toward goals, defend against anxiety—these and all our other ways of going at things *are* our selves.

Our language invites us to think in terms of subjects that act in various ways. We easily accept that lightning flashes, although, of course, the lightning *is* the flashing. In weather reports, we hear that the winds are calm, although we don't hear about what they might be doing when they are not blowing. In the same way, we are tempted to think of our I-selves as active in various ways, rather than that our activities are themselves our I-selves. I have introduced the term selving to emphasize that, as Kegan (1982) puts it in his aphoristic way, we do not speak here of the doings that our selves *do*, but of the doings that that our selves *are*.

Like Freud in his clinically near conceptions, I identify all the activities he included in *das Ich* (ego) and *das Es* (id) (as well as those of the superego) as self activities. Freud did not propose an *Ich* that does ego things or an *Es* that does id things: The activities themselves are *das Ich* and *das Es*—they are our I-selves. We are selving when we raise our children according to old internal working models, experience a disappointing test grade as "I'm fat!", understand our spending habits as matters of balance, or imagine ourselves golfing with Tiger Woods.

Our me-selves are our self representations. They are not objectively accurate perceptual inputs modified in various ways by dynamic forces; they are structured throughout by our dynamic I-schemes. They do not begin as the self pole of fused self–other units. Self representations, like object representations, begin as inchoate aspects of dynamic I-schemes. In clinical work, when self and other are not differentiated, we will not observe representations of self and other merged with one another. Rather, the less self and other are differentiated, the more we will observe only interaction modes themselves (urges, affect storms, or, perhaps, Winnicott's (1971) "going on being") with little or no articulation at all of self and other.

We structure our self and object representations as we integrate and differentiate our dynamic I-schemes. By about age two they ordinarily achieve sufficient organization to make them, in Piaget's terms, permanent objects. Throughout our lives they grow in stability and complexity as we broaden our experience in new relationships, whether within our families and friendship circles, in the course of travel, or as we engage the perspectives of science, philosophy, or literature.

At any moment our self (and object) representations reflect exactly the structure and the content of the dynamic I-schemes then in play. Davies and Frawley's (1994) abuse patients may initially reexperience early abusive situations as global nightmare events, with no articulation at all of either self or other. In his minimal sense of his separateness from me, Gary could call me Mr. Knuckles, although only he was male, and only he was raising his fist. For Greenson's (1958) patient, his loved friend was a different person when he was angry at him. My patient Ms. F could, for a moment at least, defend herself against my words by making me a transparency, a photographic negative, without the substantial physicality that is the product of mental–physical differentiation. In happier development, a girl might establish stable and complex self representations that reflect her ways of taking pride in her academic accomplishments, her bodily pleasures in her swimming and tennis skills, her growing friendliness toward her mother, or her ambivalent excitement about her ability to attract male attention.

An Agentic Self

The I-self is a self of personal motivations, not impersonal functions. Every perception, thought, feeling, and action is agentic. We move away from the Enlightenment ideal of a rational mind that is independent of the subjective. All our mental activities, however complexly attuned to our worlds, are subjective. All are agentic. All are selving.

Although all our activities are agentic, we may or may not have a *sense* of agency in them. Researchers believe that they can observe agentic infant activity from the very earliest periods of life. At three days of age, babies adjust their rate of nursing to make music play (DeCasper and Carstens, 1981). Video-tape data from three- to four-month-old-infants suggest that, in naturalistic infant–adult play, babies regulate their own activity and their interactions differently with different partners (Beebe et al., 1997). In the cross-modal attunements that become prominent at about nine months they take into account, and respond to, another's subjective state (Stern, 1985). We know little, yet, about the earliest development of a baby's own *sense* of agency in its activities. The most widely accepted marker occurs around age two. Then, with Erikson (1956), we might phrase young children's sense of identity as "I am what I will," as they test the

powers of their willing, the dangers of willfulness, and the pleasures of being willing.

In later life, to the extent that people's ways of going at
things are global, with only limited integration and differentiation of their I-schemes, their *sense* of agency might be absent or
unstable. A woman might, as in Loewald's (1976) example, feel
an "urge" to kill her child that is altogether ego alien or experience an "attack" of panic or a "wave of anxiety" with no sense
that the contributing feelings and impulses are her own. People
may have a feeling of being immersed in an activity rather than
being actively engaged in it. Looking at a Rorschach inkblot,
they may have a sense that they are simply reporting what is
there rather than actively constructing an image.

With somewhat greater differentiation, people might attribute
agency to themselves or another in radical fluctuations within a
single global interaction pattern. When Ms. F turned me into a
pattern of light and shade, she almost immediately felt herself to
be the unreal one and me the one with power. Just before Gary
called me Mr. Knuckles, it was he who was furiously threatening
me. The abuse patients of Davies and Frawley (1994) might have
experienced themselves at one moment as helpless children with
an idealized therapist but then, quite suddenly, have been the
abusive adult with the helpless child/therapist.

It is in the course of development or clinical change that we
increasingly achieve a sense of that aliveness that comes with a
sense of our own agency. We commit ourselves to relationships
rather than finding ourselves in them. We recognize that our
feeling of envy is our own, to be contended with as we might.
We are able to know that our decision to take a day off is ours,
not forced on us by circumstance.

A Self of I-Experiencing and
Its Absence

In chapter 1, I proposed taking the presence of personal agency
and the individual's sense of "I" as the two criteria for identify-

ing activities as self. Of the two, I held agency to be primary: all our activities are personally motivated but not all carry a sense of I-ness. But if I also argue that agentic activity may or may not be accompanied by a *sense* of agency, can I posit that I-ness and agency are interchangeable terms, both referring to the presence of personal motivation, and carrying a *sense* of I-ness or agency to the extent that our I-schemes are integrated and differenti-ated? I am inclined to believe so. At the least, it is probably safe to agree with Russell (1996) that a sense of I-ness is *coordinate to* a sense of agency. To take that conservative position leaves the way open to consider the two in the context of their separate domains of discussion and defer conclusions about their equiv-alence for the present.

In the I-self view, a sense of I-ness does not depend, as Freud would have it, on the person's transition from body-bound experience to engagements with the external world of objects (*Ich* experience). We interact with our worlds from the begin-ning of life; all our I-schemes reflect self–world engagements. Our activities, however, carry a *sense* of I-ness to the extent that we have integrated our I-schemes into complex and layered net-works whose self and nonself aspects are differentiated and whose mental aspects can be activated independently of their bodily ones and in the absence of the actual occurrences to which they refer.

In first-person experiencing, we are self aware. We have a sense of ourselves at the center of our lives. We experience our feelings as our own: a "scared feeling" does not permeate the entire lion-in-my-room-at-night event; a "pensive mood" does not suffuse a whole pictured interaction. We act, rather than being overwhelmed by a "need" or an "urge." We can hold in mind two conflicting ways of going about things (perhaps our ways of idealizing and scorning our therapist) and work toward their integration. We place ourselves in autobiographical time, with a sense of our present and our past and of their respective places in our anticipation of the future.

We sense ourselves to be living in an internal world. It is a world of our own individual selves distinct from others. It is a world of pri-vacy, of experiencing that we share with others at our discretion.

These internal worlds of I-experience are not the product of internalization, the transposition of an external activity or relationship into intrapsychic space. We establish and enlarge them as we differentiate the mental and physical aspects of our I-schemes. In this differentiation perspective, our sense of I-ness is not restricted to an internal world of mental activity. Rather, the differentiation of the mental and physical allows us to act mentally with or without the physical. We can imagine ourselves flying with Peter Pan or daydream about being a tennis champion with no physical involvement at all. In a "trial action" we can plan dinner at a restaurant, but our sense of I-ness is by no means diminished as we put that plan into action. We can watch a comedy with or without the physical concomitant of laughing.

We can flexibly integrate the mental and physical in such activities as metaphoric thought. With a secure differentiation of our inner and outer worlds, we can construct a metaphor that fully takes into account not only our ways of interpreting events but also the relevant physical actualities. Grasping can be more than a sensorimotor event; it can allude to our ways of being greedy for money. Balance, now more than a scheme for standing upright, can speak to issues of emotional balance or the administration of justice. To say "You can't have your cake and eat it too" is not an invitation to dessert, but a way of underscoring the consequences of choice.

With every increment of growth in our internal worlds, we enlarge our experience of the physical world in all its substantiality. We can know that neither our own bodies nor those of others can become ghostly and unreal. We are unlikely to report Rorschach images in which a person sits on an invisible chair or, like Gary when he was expecting to see his parents emerge from the elevator, be terrified at seeing "nothingness." The world can seem, in Balint's (1955) terms, a friendly expanse rather than a horrid, empty space. We do not live with the terrified sense Ogden (1986) decribes, that we might disappear without a trace in unbounded space, or as Ms. G felt it, of being balanced on a tightrope, fearful always of falling into a selfless, boundaryless void.

The absence of a sense of I-ness does not represent a retreat from the external world. We do not relegate experiences to an unconscious divorced from our self–world engagements. As in Davies's (1996) "relational unconscious," experience without a sense of I-ness (id experience) occurs in our active interactions with our worlds. Such interactions are ego alien, without psychic reality, not because they are eruptions from a primordial unconscious, but because they are, for the moment or for longer periods, isolated from our current ways of going about things.

Although we refer to experiences without a sense of I-ness as ego alien or disavowed, the absence of a sense of I-ness cannot be rectified by a simple agreement that a particular thought, feeling, or action is one's own. Activities lacking a sense of I-ness are structured in ways sharply different from first-person experiencing. They occur in global, discrete, I-scheme constellations whose self–other and mental–physical aspects are differentiated in no more than rudimentary ways. Their characteristics are those which, in relational perspectives, have been ascribed to part-self–part-object experience forms and which Freud attributed to the id.

To the extent that our I-scheme constellations are not integrated, we can have little or no sense of either I-ness or agency. Self and other are part-selves and part-objects, defined and redefined with every change in mood or event. With little sense of ourselves as actively feeling and thinking persons, we have equally little sense of others as having their own thoughts and feelings.

When the mental and physical aspects of our I-schemes are at best minimally differentiated, we have little capacity for thought independent of action. Unable to express self–world engagements in exclusively mental and verbal terms, we enact them. We have little sense of ourselves as interpreting our experience or examining it from various perspectives. Metaphor becomes symbolic equation. In the naive realism that Freud ascribed to the id, we accept as reality whatever occurs to us.

It is in the course of integrating these isolated I-scheme constellations with the larger dynamic networks of our I-selves that we achieve an increasing sense of our own centrality in our experience. In the course of this integration and the resulting self–other differentiations, we move from part-self–part-object to whole-self–whole-object experience. In coordinate mental–physical differentiations, our I-scheme experiencing loses the characteristics Freud attributed to the id and, with the achievement of a sense of I-ness, it attains those he ascribed to the ego.

A Constructivist Self

The dynamic self is the self of meaning making. The concept of the I-self does not take the objectivist view that classical psychoanalysis holds: that there is a rational structure to reality independent of the beliefs of any particular people and that these objective realities, accurately registered in the mind, are distorted in various ways by the (subjective) drives. Instead, in the I-self view, subjectivity pervades *all* experience: I-schemes—our ways of encoding our experience—are personally motivated. The meanings we make depend fundamentally on our beliefs and purposes.

In the I-self view, however, to say that we *make* meaning does not imply that any interpretation of events is as good as any other. Gergen (1991) takes the contrary position. He argues that in these postmodern times we can no longer sustain the presumption that individual minds operate as mirrors of external reality. Therefore, standards of accuracy can no longer apply. Interpretation is a matter of perspective, and any perspective is as good as any other. We cannot concern ourselves with truth, but only with various meanings.

From a psychoanalytic perspective, Spence (1982) takes a similar view. He argues that we must give up the objectivist view that objects and events are accurately registered in our minds and can be recovered in the course of analytic work. We must recognize that, although patients' memories and associations may be structured by events in the past, we cannot know those events. In our work with patients, we should ignore such memories. We should not attend to "historical truth," but should instead develop a narrative truth, a life story constructed together by patient and therapist. Its acceptability should be judged not on the basis of its accuracy in relation to actual events but on its coherence and esthetic value as a narrative.

The form of constructivism proposed here rejects these views. It suggests that our every interpretation of events reflects both the actualities *of* which we are making meaning and the I-scheme constellations (codes, templates) *by* which we do so. Throughout our lives, we test the adequacy of our interpretations, not only as coherent stories or for their esthetic value, but as they meet the requirements of actuality as we know it. A nursing infant establishes its nursing scheme in interaction with its mother. Every nursing success and failure (the infant grasps or fails to grasp the breast or bottle) tells the infant directly about the adequacy of its ways of encoding the nursing situation. Children between the ages of four and eight years establish interpretive schemes of "lunch at nursery school" or "going to the zoo" in their first encounter with the activity and modify them in subsequent episodes to accommodate the variations they discover. In later experience, we might hold two conflicting perspectives in mind simultaneously (idealizing and scornful feelings toward our therapist) to examine their validity in our actual relationships to him or her.

Our encodings of events are as primitive or as sophisticated as the I-scheme constellations we bring to bear and our sense of the actualities to be encoded. In a symbolic equation that does not distinguish our interpretations from the actuality, we might reject someone's comment that "We can't have our cake and eat it too" with the scornful assertion that we are not hungry at the moment. In terrified need, Gary could imagine that the Emersons could make his Parents' Visit possible, although in actuality they could not. With wide experience and sophisticated patterns for encoding data, we might propose such meaning-making patterns as black holes, the double helix, or the unconscious and, with these new ways of encoding events, revolutionize the ways we make meaning of our worlds.

In this view, we do not accept the primacy of the actuality of an objective external world and our subjective interpretations as no more than drive-based distortions to be resolved. In every activity, people balance their interpretive activities and their attention to actuality. In symbolic play, where interpretation properly predominates, a doll can be a baby or a broomstick a horse, but when we make a budget the actualities of financial needs must dominate. Gary, overbalancing in the interpretive direction, anticipated that he could have his Parents' Visit even without his parents, though in actuality he could not. Over-balancing in the other direction, a person might have no sense at all that he is interpreting his experience: he accepts whatever occurs to him as the reality.

We might suggest, only a little fancifully, that the objectivist conception Freud accepted and such constructivist reactions against it as those of Gergen (1991) and Spence (1982) reflect two directions of imbalance in the relations of interpretation and actuality. Freud's conception overbalances on the side of actuality: subjective interpretation of events is no more than a drive-based distortion of perception-based real-world actualities. The formulations of Gergen and Spence overbalance on the other side: interpretation is everything; we have no actuality against which to test it.

A Bodily Self

Walter Kaufmann (1980), professor of philosophy at Princeton until his death in 1980, placed Freud with Goethe and Nietzsche as the three major contributors to the Western world's discovery of the mind. Freud's signal contribution, Kaufmann argues, is that he transcended the dualism of body and mind that had plagued European thought from the time of the classical Greek philosophers. Kaufmann suggests that the essay "On Nature," attributed to Goethe, so profoundly affected Freud because it brought him to the realization that he need not choose between his inclinations toward philosophy (mind) and toward medicine (body) in his choice of career. The mind itself is part of the body, and, moreover, to study it as an aspect of our bodily selves does not require its reduction to physiological or chemical processes that deny the mystery, beauty, and complexity of human experience.

Nevertheless, even in Freud's work, the Enlightenment view that valued mind over body, and rationality and objectivity over affect and subjectivity, formed a pervasive undercurrent. Freud posited the origins of the mind in bodily experiences, but he suggested that mental development begins with the child's turn from body-bound experience to the external world. Body-based experience forms are subjective and irrational (the primary processes) and, in the course of development, give way to reason based on our orientations to the external world of objective reality (the secondary processes). The internal worlds of mature functioning are the products of internalization, the transposition of (more primitive) bodily activities to the new (more advanced) arena of mental life. Affects are derivatives of bodily drives whose effects must be overcome to permit true rationality.

Loewald (1980), still within the framework of Freud's drive theory, takes a more celebratory view of our bodily experience. The life of the body, he suggests, is a life of

> bodily needs and habits and functions, kisses and excrements and intercourse, tastes and smells and sights, body noises and sensations, caresses and punishments, tics and gait and movements, facial expression, the penis and the vagina and the tongue and arms and hands and feet and legs and hair, pain and pleasure, physical excitement and lassitude, violence and bliss [p. 125].

The I-self conception takes a perspective not unlike Loewald's. In this view, as in Freud's, our minds are ineluctably grounded in our bodily activities. In the I-self view, however, these are not body-bound activities in which the infant is oblivious to its surround: they are bodily interactions with the world. Our minds are bodily minds, our "thoughts" patterned by our bodily actions. The interaction patterns that structure our minds, however, are not schemes of impersonal, physiologically based urges, but of personally motivated actions. They are not exclusively unrealistic but are based on infants' active and adaptive interactions with their worlds. They are not bodily schemes devoid of mental content but are psychomotor schemes of which the mental and bodily aspects are not yet differentiated.

Our capacities for intrapsychic experience do not entail a turn away from the bodily, an internalization that transposes physical experience to a mental arena. Rather, we establish these capacities by the differentiation of the mental and physical aspects of our I-schemes. We do not replace the physical with the mental: we become able to act mentally with or without bodily sensation and action. We can feel tenderly with or without caresses and kisses, think about food with or without smelling and tasting it, and have opinions with or without revealing them in our facial expressions.

Every mental–physical differentiation elaborates not only the subtlety and complexity of our ways of thinking and feeling but, equally, the sophistication of our bodily experiencing. We refine our food preferences of infancy and childhood toward increasing subtlety of taste in food and wine. In the ways we move, a primary identification of "walking Daddy's walk" can become complexly integrated into our own personal gait.

In optimum circumstances, the bodily aspects of our experience do not provide merely a primitive and largely hidden counterpoint to our "mature" experience modes; rather, they enrich our ways of selving throughout our lives. A young father's paternal feelings toward his newborn are not more primitive if he also cradles the baby in his arms. Our sense of a painting's beauty is enriched rather than diminished by the subtleties of our bodily reactions to it. Our appreciation of a piece of music is not less sophisticated if we are members of the choir. Our ways of loving are not more subtle or elevated if we refrain from expressing them in bodily ways.

A Self of Unity and Complexity

The I-self is not a fundamentally inborn self. Neither is it a self of discontinuous self states with little or no cohesion.

The first view is central to classical psychoanalysis: our selves (*das Ich*) are rooted in the drive-based structures of the id. This view is apparent in Winnicott's (1971) conception of the "true self." As Bollas (1989) develops that idea, the infant has its own, intrinsic "form," a personal idiom, embedded in the design of its inherited disposition and its own cognitive abilities. From a self psychological perspective, Tolpin (1986) speaks of the "givens" that interact with experience to form the self. They provide an outline or range of outlines that will consolidate and be filled in to constitute the self of later life.

Mitchell (1991), taking the second, increasingly popular view, suggests that our selves are plural or manifold organizations, composed of many discrete configurations. We are, in a fundamental sense, quite different persons at different times or with different people. Our sense of the continuity of our selves is illusory.

In Gergen's (1991) view, this nonintegration of self reflects the predominant self organization of our time. We tend to have no enduring core of deep and indelible character. The centered will of a single ego is vanishing. We exhilarate in the the multiplicity of our selves. We live a protean life style of equally real but mutually exclusive aspects of the self. self awareness and self reflection are disappearing. Coherence and contradiction cease to matter. We swim in ever-shifting, concatenating, and contentious currents of being.

In the I-self view, the cohesion of our selves is neither inborn nor illusory; it is a developmental achievement. We begin, in infancy, with many discrete self states, constellations of I-schemes representing our various ways of going about things in our worlds. Throughout our lives, we integrate our I-schemes into increasingly complex and subtle networks of self aspects. At any point in our experience, our selves are both unified and multifarious: some groups of I-scheme constellations form secure and largely permanent unities; others are more loosely integrated; and still others are actively excluded from the larger networks of our ways of selving.

This view does not celebrate a manifold self of discrete self states. In the I-self view, it is with the integration of I-self constellations that we achieve an increasing sense of I-ness. With that integration, we attain a sense of ourselves as individuals in relation to others, with their own ways of thinking and feeling. We live in a solidly real world of physical actualities. We move beyond global "enactments" toward possibilities for thought independent of action, for metaphor and the metaphoric projection that Johnson finds at the heart of our mental activity.

The integration of self states, in this view, does not result in a bland uniformity of experience, an "averaging" that loses the exhilaration of difference. On the contrary, it is through the integration of I-schemes that we achieve richness of experiencing. If Deutsch's (1942) painter patient had been able to integrate the two very different approaches of her teachers, she might have established her own distinctively personal style of painting rather than moving from style to style in an imitative and fundamentally empty way. If a man, in the course of mourning, becomes integratively aware of his fragmentary, intense senses of himself as a playboy, a zombie dead to all that is good, or a computer brain with no need for sentiment, his ways of selving are enriched rather than averaged into an impoverished blandness.

The kaleidoscopic variety that can occur when one's self is defined and redefined with every shift in motivation or feeling might suggest an admirable complexity. More extended observation, however, suggests a less attractive alternative. Deutsch's

(1942) painter patient was accepted as a brilliant student by each teacher in turn, but in each case the teacher's initial excitement turned to disappointment as the student's adoption of the teacher's style remained imitative, without the individuality that integration with her other ways of painting might bring. In a patient such as Greenson's (1958), a limited emotional complexity might become evident as a loved person becomes a different person for him when he is angry at him.

Notions of manifold self experience, of protean life styles, or of swimming in ever-shifting currents of being might suggest an excitingly variegated and adventurous life. The I-self concept sounds a less happy note—the possibility that selving in relatively unintegrated constellations of I-schemes may also be painfully disjunctive. When our ways of encoding experience are not integrated, unexpected events may leave us, for the moment at least, altogether without ways of making sense of what is happening and with no sense of our own selves and our place in an ambient world. Then, our worlds might seem not as friendly expanses of unlimited possibility, but, rather, horrid empty spaces. In Gary's painful terms, we might feel ourselves "like not being attached to anything . . . like a machine with all its wires loose . . . like a machine not working but you're still alive." Like the competent young Ms. G, we might feel ourselves constantly on a tightrope, anxiously organizing our days, fearful of falling yet again into a selfless, boundaryless void.

An Intersubjective Self

In the I-self perspective, we do not relate to others only as objects of drive satisfaction or frustration, as in Freud's theory. Nor are the "others" of our interactions the "objects" of object relational perspectives, object representations coordinate to our self representations. Instead, the I-self notion that our selves are networks of dynamic interaction patterns invites an intersubjective perspective largely congruent with the concept Benjamin (1988, 1995) has been developing. In the I-self form of intersubjectivity, we differentiate our own and others' parts in our interactions, not the self and object representations of self–other units. The 'others' of these differentiations are not object representations; they are dynamic constellations of perceiving, thinking, feeling, and acting that we attribute to other persons. A woman, initially having no more than a global sense of difficulties at work, might struggle to become clear about her own and her supervisor's contributions to them. A father, entangled in intensely competitive interactions with his daughter, might work hard to differentiate within them his own and his daughter's parts.

This view does not suggest, however, as Benjamin's appears to, that people progress from reacting to others as objects toward interacting with them as subjects. It suggests, instead, that progress in clinical work and development occurs *within* our intersubjective ways of understanding our worlds: we do not progress from subject–object relationships to subject–subject ones rather, we move from primitive subject–subject relationships to more mature ones. It seems likely, for example, that, as Hoffman (1991) suggests, patients in clinical analysis are likely to attribute subjectivity to their analysts from the very beginning. They might "experience the analyst's investment in being the analyst, in being the one who understands rather than the one who is understood, who is needed rather than who needs" (p. 541) From an I-self perspective, we might expect that, in the course of analysis, patients would modify their views of the analyst's subjectivity in a great number of directions as they expand their ways of encoding their patient–analytst interactions both in old patterns to be modified and in new ones that more fully reflect the actualities of those interactions.

Observations of development, too, seem to suggest that from early life onward we engage in forms of intersubjectivity rather than subject–object relationships. Stern (1985) convincingly argues that, in the cross-modal affect attunements common in infant–mother interactions at about 9 to 15 months, infants accurately perceive and respond to their mothers' subjective states. In summarizing "theory of mind" studies, Fonagy and Target (1996) suggest that, even before that time, infants' behaviors (pointing and looking at the caregiver or checking back for the caregiver's reaction to strange situations) imply awareness of other people's minds. And, by about three or four years of age, Wellman's (1990) studies suggest, children readily attribute goals, desires, and beliefs both to themselves and to others.

We expect that in later life, if self–other differentiation is little more than rudimentary, people might attribute subjectivity to others in various primitive ways, rather than reacting to them as objects without their own perceptions and feelings. In her story-tellers' most limited attribution of feelings to characters in pictured situations, for example, Thompson (1986) observed not subject–object relationships but attributions of feeling to the situation as a whole or in unstable ways to both interacting persons: an entire pictured event might be "filled with anxiety . . . [or] . . . could involve the interrelationship between them [the two pictured persons] . . . or maybe it's hard for her to tell him, or vice versa" (p. 219). The subjectivity ascribed to the other might shift radically from one moment to another, as when Gary felt his parents to be loving and caring (coming to taking him home), but, in a moment, as abandoning him (missing his Parents' Visit). Feelings and intentions attributed to the other might be narrowly complementary to those of the self and fluctuate in self–other reversals within a global interaction mode, as when Ms. F imperiously turned me into a negative but almost instantly felt herself the helpless victim of my powerful negation. Only at higher levels of I-scheme integration and differentiation, will we, in this view, find the forms of intersubjectivity for which Benjamin (1995) uses that term: "The other who is truly perceived as outside, distinct from our mental field of operations" and who is "a separate and equivalent center of self" (p. 29).

Moreover, the I-self framework suggests that our capacity for a sense of our own subjectivity (of I-ness) is no greater than our ability to ascribe subjectivity to others. If, as this conception implies, we establish our sense of our own self and that of others together by differentiation within our I-schemes, we can expect that our capacity for a sense of our own subjectivity (I-ness) in an activity will be matched exactly by our capacity for sensing the other as a center of selving. If we have little sense that we are thinking our thoughts and feeling our feelings, we are likely to have equally little sense of others as thinking, feeling persons. Only when we can recognize that we have a point of view of our own will we be able to assume that the other also has a particular perspective. As Loewald's (1976) patient became aware that her own feelings toward her husband and father had patterned the urge to kill her child, she also gained an increasing sense of her husband and father as centers of thinking and feeling specific to them.

The view that in any interpersonal activity our sense of I-ness can be only as complex and multifaceted as our sense of the other's hints at some aspects of empathy in both social and clinical situations. It suggests that the subtlety and range of our capacities for empathy with another at any moment will reflect the breadth and depth of our present engagement in the encounter. Might this view suggest too that clinical work, with its constant demand for enlarging our empathic capacities, also provides a source of joy in the coordinate expansion and increased depth of our own sense of I-ness?

A Self Both Individual and Relational

The I-self perspective suggests that our sense of individuality (I-ness) and our capacities for relationship develop together. It does not share the widely expressed fear that a relational perspective within psychoanalytic psychology must undermine psychoanalytic attention to ourselves as individuals with our own internal worlds and psychic structures.

For Modell (1993) this concern is central: "In emphasizing the vital significance of the private self, I am striving to correct a current bias that views the self as nearly exclusively a social self" (p. 4). Wilson (1995) suggests that to commit oneself to relational perspectives is "to dispense with psychic structure itself" In relational analyses, he suggests

> the give-and-take of relationship factors is the priority, and the mind disappears from view. The interpretations and the specification of conflicts that are out of awareness become superseded by the mutual search for authentic contact, as insight is superseded by relationship factors as primary mutative factors in analysis [p. 19].

In the same vein, Gergen (1991) argues that our postmodern perspectives replace the notion of a fundamentally interior, autonomous individual by a view in which "the self vanishes fully into a stage of relatedness" (p. 17). The idea of an intentional, rational agent begins to fray. There is no essential self, no internal core. We cease to believe in a self independent of the relations in which we are embedded.

Benjamin (1995) argues strongly that we must neither exclude the intersubjective in a focus on the intrapsychic nor minimize the intrapsychic in a concern for the intersubjective. Her own interests focus centrally on the intersubjective, but she argues, in ways congruent with the I-self perspective, that, in our commitment to a relational model, we must not lose all that we have learned in the traditional intrapsychic one. In this context she seems to suggest that maintaining a distinction between them is no more than a heuristic, a device useful at our present stage of theory development. We should attend to the tensions between the two models in the hope of an eventual resolution.

At other times, Benjamin appears to suggest that the distinction between the intrapsychic and the interpersonal is an actual one, not merely a theoretical one. She speaks of the intrapsychic and the intersubjective as two dimensions or categories of experience. In our thinking, she emphasizes, we must preserve the tension between the two, rather than accepting possibly spurious resolutions of the contraditions among antithetical elements. She develops the idea that that we relate to others both as objects of identification and projection (intrapsychically) and as independent objects (intersubjectively). It is here that the I-self conception differs from hers.

In the I-self view, the establishment and growth of our individual selves and of our capacities for relationship are coordinate developments. In every I-scheme integration, we expand our internal worlds of autonomy and privacy. We more fully integrate the networks of our I-schemes to form the stable structures of a core self, capable of perceiving, thinking, and feeling in ways independent of our immediate situations. Simultaneously, in the same integration processes, we become more capable of mature relationships, of accepting our interaction partners as distinct from ourselves, as centers of their own individual ways of selving.

Capacities for solitude and relationship are not at opposite poles of experience. They are intimately related throughout our lives. Our capacity for independence and solitude is learned in the intimacies of relationship and depends on them for its flowering. In his inimitable way, Winnicott (1971) suggests that infants learn solitude in the absence of the present mother, that is, when they play alone in the presence of their mothers. The attachment literature seems to support the notion that when children are securely attached they are able to sustain their capacity for solitary play in brief absences from the mother. And Coates, Friedman, and Wolfe's (1991) seminal studies of gender identity disorders seem to suggest that young boys' abilities to achieve individual and sexual differentiation from their mothers may be imperiled if the mother–child relationship is disrupted (because, e.g., of the mother's illness or a personal crisis) at the height of the boys' efforts to achieve these forms of independence of and separation from her.

Conversely, in an important sense, throughout our lives we are solitary even within relationships. In ordinarily mature interactions with others, our individuality does not disappear. In every interpersonal engagement, each participant brings his or her own ways of encoding what is going on to the interchange. Winnicott's (1971) notion that in infant–mother relationships there is no infant and no mother, but only an infant–mother unit can serve to emphasize the intimacy of that relationship, but, as Ogden (1986) points out, the mother must also function outside this unit. In therapeutic engagements, as Aron (1991) emphasizes, patient and therapist have their own individual and separate parts. And Ogden's (1995) notion of "the analytic third" is experienced through the individual personality systems of analyst and analysand and is therefore not an identical feeling for each.

In the I-self view, the more people are capable of intimacy, concern, and relationship throughout their lives, the more they will be capable of active, productive, or quietly recuperative solitude. Conversely, incompleteness in one will be related to incompleteness in the other. An adolescent girl struggling to free herself from an intrusive mother might furiously demand to be left alone and yet find solitude difficult, permeated by internal arguments in the absence of the actual mother. An adult who demands solitude as a liberation from the imprisonment of intimacy may find in that solitude a tense and angry fear of interruption by the other or a helpless oversensitivity to the possible ringing of the telephone.

It is when we are capable of mature relationships that solitude does not diminish our enjoyment of being with others; our contentment in relationships is not contrary to our enjoyment of solitude. It is when we have established a fundamentally interior, autonomous self that we can most fully engage in the give-and-take of relationships. Our capacity for authentic contact with others is enhanced to the extent that we have establishied the internal core of an independent self. Only when we have a sense of I-ness and agency in our activities will we be able to immerse ourselves fully in the intersubjectivity of interdependence.

A Possible Self?

The I-self conception is one possible way we might imagine our dynamic selves. It has been a pleasure to develop it in this

exhilarating time of ferment in the construction of psychoanalytic perspectives. The long hegemony of ego psychology,
with its firmly objectivist base, seems to be giving way to relational perspectives with a largely constructivist bent. Our
challenge today is to construct a relational framework for psychoanalysis that can accommodate the rich heritage of observation and conceptualization that derives from Freud's
explorations, from ego psychology, and from other psychoanalytic perspectives.

The idea of a dynamic I-self seems to me one that can contribute to this process. It is a thoroughly relational conception:
the very structures of our I-selves are interaction schemes. It
takes a particular constructivist position, one that gives weight
both to our structures of understanding and to the actualities of
which we are trying to make sense. In important ways it returns
to Freud's clinically near view that our minds are dynamic
structures of personal motivation, not impersonal functions: *das
Ich*, those ways of going about things which we experience as I;
das Es, those which we experience as ego alien.

In the belief that any reconceptualization, if it is to be useful,
must speak to major issues in these central streams of psychoanalytic thought, I have paid particular attention to the ways this
conception might accommodate observations that have been
framed in drive theory and relational perspectives. It has been
particularly gratifying to find connections, too, to arenas of
thought and research beyond psychoanalysis. Here Piaget's
work has been central to my thinking, but beyond this, the I-self
conception appears also to be congruent with James's still useful
ideas, with current conceptions emerging from research on
infancy and child development and from insights rooted in philosophy and linguistics.

As we move toward a widely accepted relational framework
for psychoanalysis, we can expect a proliferation of theories and
part-theories. I hope that the way of thinking about our dynamic
selves presented here can be a part of these exciting developments.

REFERENCES

Abraham, K. (1921), Contributions to the theory of the anal character. In: *Selected Papers of Karl Abraham*. New York: Basic Books, 1927.

Apfelbaum, B. (1966), On ego psychology: A critique of the structural approach to psychoanalytic theory. *International Journal of Psycho-Analysis*. 47: 451–475.

Aron, L. (1991). The patient's experience of the analyst's subjectivity. *Psychoanalytic Dialogues*, 1: 29–51.

Balint, M. (1955), Friendly expanses—Horrid empty spaces. *International Journal of Psycho-Analysis*, 36:225–241.

Beebe, B., Lachmann, F. & Jaffe, J. (1997), Mother–infant interaction structures and presymbolic self and object representations. *Psychoanalytic Dialogues*, 7:133–182.

Benjamin, J. (1988), *The Bonds of Love: Psychoanalysis, Feminism, and the Problem of Domination*. New York: Pantheon.

Benjamin, J. (1995), *Like Subjects, Love Objects*. New Haven, CT: Yale University Press.

Bollas, C. (1989), *Forces of Destiny: Psychoanalysis and the Human Idiom*. London: Free Association Books.

Bruner, J. B. (1992), *Acts of Meaning*. Cambridge, MA: Harvard University Press.

Bruner, J. B. (1993), Loyal opposition and the clarity of dissent. *Psychoanalytic Dialogues*, 3:11–20.

Coates, S., Friedman, R. W. & Wolfe, S. (1991), The etiology of boyhood gender identity disorder: A model for integrating temperament, development, and psychodynamics. *Psychoanalytic Dialogues*, 1:481–523.

Cohn, D. (1992), Freud's case histories and the question of fictionality. In: J. H. Smith (ed.), *Telling Facts: History and Narration in Psychoanalysis*. Baltimore, MD: Johns Hopkins University Press.

Davies, J. M. (1996), Linking the "pre-analytic" with the postclassical. *Contemporary Psychoanalysis*, 32:553–576.

Davies, J. M. & Frawley, M. G. (1994), *Treating the Adult Survivor of Child-hood Sexual Abuse*. New York: Basic Books.

DeCasper, A. J. & Carstens, A. A. (1981), Contingencies of stimulation: Effects on learning and emotion in neonates. *Infant Behavior and Development*, 4:19–35.

Demos, E. V. (1992), The early organization of the psyche. In: J. W. Barron, M. N. Eagle, & D. L Wolitzky (eds.), *Interface of Psychoanalysis and Psychology*. Washington, DC: American Psychological Association, pp. 200–232.

Deutsch, H. (1942), Some forms of emotional disturbance and their relationship to schizophrenia. *Psychoanalytic Quarterly*, 2:301–321.

Douglas, A. (1995), *Terrible Honesty*. New York: Farrar, Straus & Giroux.

Dreyfus, H. L. (1991), *Being in the World: A Commentary on Heidegger's Being and Time, Division l*. Cambridge, MA: MIT Press.

Eagle, M. (1984a), *Recent Developments in Psychoanalysis*. Cambridge, MA: Harvard University Press.

Eagle, M. (1984b), Geha's vision of psychoanalysis as fiction. *International Forum for Psychoanalysis*, 1:341–362.

Erikson, E. H. (1956), The problem of ego identity. *Journal of the American Psychoanalytic Association*, 4:56–121.

Fairbairn, W. R. D. (1952), *An Object-Relations Theory of the Personality*. New York: Basic Books.

Fast, I. (1969), Concrete and abstract thought: An alternative formulation. *Journal of Projective Techniques and Personality Assessment*, 33:331–335.

Fast, I. (ed.) (1985), *Event Theory: A Piaget-Freud Integration*. Hillsdale, NJ: Lawrence Erlbaum Associates.

Fast, I., Marsden, K. G., Cohen, L., Heard, H. & Kruse, S. (1996), Self as subject: A formulation and an assessment strategy. *Psychiatry*, 59:34–47.

Fitzpatrick, C. J. (1985), Children's development out of event-bound conceptions of their emotion. In: I. Fast (ed.) *Event Theory: A Piaget-Freud Integration*. Hillsdale, NJ: Lawrence Erlbaum Associates.

Flavell, J. H. (1963), *The Developmental Psychology of Jean Piaget*. Princeton, NJ: Van Nostrand.

Fonagy, P. (1995), Playing with reality: The development of psychic reality and its malfunction in borderline personalities. *International Journal of Psycho-Analysis*, 76:39–45.

Fonagy, P. Steele, M., Steele, H., Leigh, T. Kennedy, R. & Target, M. (1993), The predictive specificity of Mary Main's Adult Attachment Interview: Implications for psychodynamic theories of normal and pathological development. Presented at conference on "John Bowlby's Attachment Theory: Historical, Clinical and Social Significance," Toronto.

Fonagy, P. & Target, M. (1996). Playing with reality: I. Theory of mind and the normal development of psychic reality. *International Journal of Psycho-Analysis*, 77:217–233.

Fraiberg, S. (1969), Libidinal object constancy and mental representation. *The Psychoanalytic Study of the Child*, 24:9–47. New York: International Universities Press.

Freud, S. (1900), The interpretation of dreams *Standard Edition*, 4 & 5. London: Hogarth Press, 1953.

Freud, S. (1911), Formulations on the two principles of mental functioning. *Standard Edition*, 12:218–226. London: Hogarth Press, 1958.

Freud, S. (1914a), Remembering, repeating and working-through. *Standard Edition*, 12:147–156. London: Hogarth Press, 1958.

Freud, S. (1914b) On narcissism: An introduction. *Standard Edition*, 14:75–102. London: Hogarth Press, 1957.

Freud, S. (1918), From the history of an infantile neurosis. *Standard Edition*, 17:1–122. London: Hogarth Press, 1955.

Freud, S. (1921), Group psychology and the analysis of the ego. *Standard Edition*, 18:108–143. London: Hogarth Press, 1955.

Freud, S. (1925), An autobiographical study. *Standard Edition*, 20:3–74. London: Hogarth Press, 1959.

Gergen, K. J. (1991), *The Saturated Self*. New York: Basic Books.

Gill, M. M. (1967), The primary process. In: R. R. Holt (ed.) *Motives and Thought*. New York: International Universities Press.

Goldberg, S., Muir, R. & Kerr, J. (eds.) (1995), *Attachment Theory*. Hillsdale, NJ: The Analytic Press.

Goldstein, K. (1944), Methodological approach to the study of schizophrenic thought disorder. In: J. S. Kasanin, (ed.) *Language and thought in Schizophrenia*. Berkeley: University of California Press.

Greenson, R. R. (1958), On screen defenes, screen hunger and screen identity. *Journal of the American Psychoanalytic Association*, 6:242–262.

Gruber, H. E. & Voneche, J. J. (eds.) (1977), *The Essential Piaget*. New York: Basic Books.

Hanfmann, E. & Kasanin, J. (1952), Conceptual thinking in schizophrenia. *Nervous and Mental Disease Monographs*, 67. New York: Nervous Mental Disease.

Hartmann, H. (1950), Comments on the psychoanalytic theory of the ego. *The Psychoanalytic Study of the Child*, 5:74–96. New York: International Universities Press.

Hartmann, H., Kris, E. & Loewenstein, R. M. (1947), Comments on the formation of psychic structure. *The Psychoanalytic Study of the Child* 2:11–38. New York: International Universities Press.

Hoffman, I. Z. (1991), Discussion: Toward a social-constructivist view of the psychoanalytic situation. *Psychoanalytic Dialogues*, 1:74–105.

Jacobson, E. (1964), *The Self and the Object World*. New York: International Universities Press.

Jacobson, L. (1997), The soul of psychoanalysis in the modern world: Reflections on the work of Christopher Bollas. *Psychoanalytic Dialogues*, 7:81–116.

James, W. (1892), The self. In: C. Gordon & K. S. Gergen (eds.) *The Self in Interaction, Vol. l*. New York: J. Wiley, 1968.

Johnson, M. (1987), *The Body in the Mind*. Chicago: University of Chicago Press.

Karen, R. (1994), *Becoming Attached*. New York: Warner Books.

Kaufmann, W. (1980), *Discovering the Mind, Vol 2*. New York: McGraw Hill.

Kegan, R. (1982), *The Evolving Self*. Cambridge, MA: Harvard University Press.

Kernberg, O. (1966), Structural derivatives of object relationships. *International Journal of Psycho-Analysis*, 47:236–253.

Klein, G. S. (1976), *Psychoanalytic Theory: An Exploration of Essentials*. New York: International Universities Press.

Kulka, R. (1997), Quantum selfhood. *Psychoanalytic Dialogues*, 7:183–188.

Lakoff, G. & Johnson, M. (1980), *Metaphors We Live By*. Chicago: University of Chicago Press.

Lewis, M. & Brooks-Gunn, J. (1979), *Social Cognition and the Acquisition of Self*. New York: Plenum Press.

Loewald, H. W. (1971), On motivation and instinct theory. *The Psychoanalytic Study of the Child*, 26:91–127. New York: Quadrangle Press.

Loewald, H. W. (1976), Perspectives on memory. In: *Papers on psychoanalysis*. New Haven, CT: Yale University Press.

Loewald, H. W. (1977), Instinct theory, object relations, and psychic structure formation. In: *Papers on Psychoanalysis*. New Haven, CT: Yale University Press.

Loewald, H. W. (1980), In: *Papers on Psychoanalysis*. New Haven, CT: Yale University Press.

Mahler, M. S., Pine, F. & Bergman A. (1975), *The Psychological Birth of the Human Infant*. New York: Basic Books.

Main, M. (1991), Metacognitive knowledge, metacognitive monitoring, and singular (coherent) vs. multiple (incoherent) model of attachment. In: C. M. Parkes, J. Stevenson-Hinde & P Morris (eds.) *Attachment Across the Life Cycle*. London: Routledge.

Meissner, W. W, (1986), Can psychoanalysis find its self? *Journal of the American Psychoanalytic Association*, 34:379–400.

Mitchell, S. A. (1991), Contemporary perspectives on self: Toward an integration. *Psychoanalytic Dialogues*, 1:121–147.

Modell, A. H. (1968), *Object Love and Reality*. New York: International Universities Press.

Modell, A. H. (1993), *The Private Self*. Cambridge, MA: Harvard University Press.

Nelson, K. (ed.) (1986), *Event Knowledge: Structure and Function in Development*. Hillsdale, NJ: Lawrence Erlbaum Associates.

Nelson, K. (1989), *Narratives From the Crib*. Cambridge, MA: Harvard University Press.

Ogden, T. H. (1986), *The Matrix of the Mind*. Northvale, NJ: Aronson.

Ogden, T. H. (1991), An interview with Thomas Ogden. *Psychoanalytic Dialogues*, 1:361–376.

Ogden, T. H. (1995), Analyzing forms of aliveness and deadness of the transference–countertransference. *International Journal of Psycho-Analysis*, 76:695–709.

Rapaport, D., Gill, M. & Schafer, R. (1946), *Diagnostic Psychological Testing*, Vol. 2. The Menninger Clinic Monograph Series, N. 4. Chicago: Yearbook.

Rorty, R. (1993), Centers of moral gravity. *Psychoanalytic Dialogues*, 3:21–28).

Rose, S. A. & Russ, M. A. (1987), Cross-modal abilities in human infants. In: J. D. Osofsky (ed.) *Handbook of Infant Development*, New York: Wiley, pp. 318–362.

Russell, J. (1996), *Agency: Its Role in Mental Development*. Hillsdale, NJ: Lawrence Erlbaum Associates.

Sandler, J. & Rosenblatt, B (1962), The concept of the representational world. *The Psychoanalytic Study of the Child*, 17:128–145. New York: International Universities Press.

Sarbin, T. R., (ed.) (1986), *Narrative Psychology*. New York: Praeger Special Studies.

Schafer, R. (1968), *Aspects of Internalization*. New York: International Universities Press.

Schafer, R. (1976), *A New Language for Psychoanalysis*. New Haven, CT: Yale University Press.

Schafer, R. (1992), *Retelling a Life*. New York: Basic Books.

Schank, R. C. & Abelson, R. P. (1977), *Scripts, Plans, Goals, and Understanding*. Hillsdale, NJ: Lawrence Erlbaum Associates.

Searles, H. F. (1962), The differentiation between concrete and metaphorical thinking in the recovering schizophrenic patient. In: *Collected Papers in Schizophrenia and Related Subjects*. New York: International Universities Press, 1965.

Segal, H. (1957), Notes on symbol formation. *International Journal of Psycho-Analysis*, 38:391–397.

Spence, D. P. (1982), *Narrative Truth and Historical Truth*. New York: Norton.

Stern, D. N. (1985), *The Interpersonal World of the Infant*. New York: Basic Books.

Stern, D. N. (1994), One way to build a clinically relevant baby. *Infant Mental Health Journal*, 15:9–25.

Target, M. & Fonagy, P. (1996), Playing with reality: II. The development of psychic reality from a theoretical perspective. *International Journal of Psycho-Analysis*, 77:459–479.

Thompson, A. E. (1986), An object relational theory of affect maturity: Applications to the thematic apperception test. In: M. Kissen, (ed.) *Assessing Object Relations Phenomena*. New York: International Universities Press

Tolpin, M. (1986), The self and its selfobjects: A different baby. In: A. Goldberg (ed.) *Progress in Self Psychology, Vol 2*. New York: Guilford Press.

Wallace, E. R. (1984), Psychoanalysis: History-writing or storytelling? *International Forum for Psychoanalysis*, 1:315–340.

Wellman, H. (1990), *The Child's Theory of Mind*. Cambridge, MA: Bradford Books/MIT Press.

Wilson, A. (1995), Mapping the mind in relational psychoanalysis: Some critiques, questions, and conjectures. *Psychoanalytic Psychology*, 12:9–29.

Winnicott, D. W. (1963), Communicating and not communicating leading to a study of certain opposites. In: *The Maturational Process and Facilitating Environment*, New York: International Universities Press, 1965, pp. 179–192.

Winnicott, D. W. (1971), *Playing and Reality*. New York: Basic Books.

Young, L & Fast, I. (1985), Omnipotence and primary creativity in Rorschach responses: Toward a replacement of Rapaport's "distance" concept. In: I. Fast (ed.) *Event Theory: A Piaget-Freud Integration*. Hillsdale, NJ: Lawrence Erlbaum Associates.

INDEX